HYGGE PUZZLES

HYGGE
PUZZLES

Over 150 soothing puzzles
with quotes to inspire a feeling of
hygge, the Nordic philosophy of
wellness and contentment.

This edition published in 2023 by Arcturus Publishing Limited
26/27 Bickels Yard, 151–153 Bermondsey Street,
London SE1 3HA

AD005797NT

Printed in the UK

MIX
Paper | Supporting
responsible forestry
FSC® C171272

Contents

Hygge Puzzles

A wonderful collection of enjoyable puzzles and inspirations

Pronounced "hoo-ga", the Nordic concept of hygge sounds just like a warm, friendly hug. And that shouldn't come as a surprise, because this 16th-century Norwegian word is related to the English word "hug" and can be broadly defined as coziness or contentment. But that is a bit like saying watching the sunrise over the Taj Mahal is pretty. It's true, but there's so much more to it.

Hygge is an attitude of mind, a place, a feeling, an atmosphere, a way of thinking. It can envelop you like a warm blanket and infiltrate every area of your life just as the gentle aroma of hot coffee through a sunlit room might. Hygge means finding the time to appreciate the simple things in life that make you feel good; spending time with the people who matter most to you; relishing the small, gentle pleasures that can so easily be overlooked; banishing unnecessary irritations and annoyances. It teaches us that we don't have to choose between quality and quantity. If you have hygge in your life, you'll relish every moment and use all your senses, including your intuition, to make every day and every moment as happy as possible.

In fact, it's the Danes, not the Norwegians, who have taken hygge to their hearts and woven it into the fabric of their nation to such an extent that they regularly come top in the United Nations World Happiness Report. Could it be that hygge is responsible for the nation's contentment? It seems likely.

We all know that money enables us to meet our basic needs but, once those needs are met, more money doesn't inevitably lead to more happiness. Embracing hygge at the heart of your life, on the other hand—as the Danes have done—provides a much more satisfactory answer. If we search out hygge in each of the elements of our lives, there is a good chance we will find contentment at home, at the table, with friends, out and about, and even at work.

Hygge at home

The clean, minimalist simplicity of Scandi-chic interior design is the embodiment of hygge, focusing, as it does, on simplicity, practicality, and comfort. To be truly hygge, a home should be a calm refuge, with a pleasantly serene and not too vibrant decor, displaying the balance that is at the heart of hygge. A hygge home is somewhere you can totally relax, switch off, and indulge in simple pleasures, like enjoying a duvet day with a pile of cushions, an old movie, and a roaring fire; relaxing in a hot, fragrant bubble bath at the end of a long day or reading an engrossing novel or a memorable poem with the sunlight streaming through the window.

Of course, that old t-shirt and those jog pants—faded and soft from so many washes—will be your hygge outfit of choice, with the slipper socks your mother knitted for you so many years ago you can't remember. You might have some knitting of your own on the go, or perhaps sewing or tapestry, painting or drawing, or some other creative art.

Hygge at the table

To complete your perfect hygge afternoon, you might like to team your movie with a mug of steaming hot chocolate or a glass of the beverage of your choice with one or two delicious cookies or perhaps a Danish pastry or a cardamom muffin. Because food and drink can be hygge, too, especially comfort foods and things that remind you of your childhood, like chocolate cake, pancakes, and porridge.

In the kitchen, sharing the preparation and cooking of your meals will definitely increase your hygge ratings, as it not only encourages knowledge about good food and a balanced diet, it also teaches practical skills and co-operation. Why not try baking bread and enjoying that wonderful aroma of a fresh loaf straight from the oven? That's a real hygge bonus.

In restaurants and bars, the hygge menu will offer a small selection of substantial but healthy options that you can enjoy at your own pace, appreciating every mouthful. Comfortable rather than über smart, in a hygge café, everyone will switch their smartphone to silent.

Hygge with friends

Of course, the company of our family and friends is another notch on our hygge score, whether we are at home or eating out somewhere where the atmosphere is convivial and intimate. Cheerfully sharing a freshly prepared and nourishing meal, surrounded by good company, laughter, and camaraderie will enhance our well-being and underscore our sense of community and belonging.

You might enjoy cultural pursuits with your friends, too, by sharing a common interest in the movies, ballet, opera, music, or art. Sitting in front of a painting you love in a serene gallery can be totally absorbing.

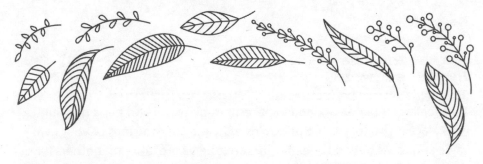

Hygge out and about

When it's time to walk the dog, anyone who embraces hygge will not worry about the weather. If it's cold, wear another layer. If it's raining, wear your boots and take an umbrella. It's not the fault of the weather if you get wet and cold; it just means you were wearing the wrong clothes. Dress for the season and for the weather you can see out of the window, the forecast can only ever be a guide.

Go for a walk in the park, around a quaint old town, or through some beautiful gardens. Ride your bike into the country or along the river, enjoy the wind in your hair and the rain on your face—relish every moment.

Stop off for a hearty brunch or tea and cakes at a café or bar where the welcome is exceptional and you can amicably discuss even religion or politics with respect for one another's opinions.

Then, back at home again, you can equally enjoy casting off all your wet and muddy clothes and sipping a cup of tea in the warm, with the dog asleep at your feet, reading the paper, and watching the rain beat against the window.

And if the weather is fine, there are just as many hygge things you can do. Take the children to the beach and be as child-like as them, splashing in the sea or building sandcastles. Spend some time digging the garden, growing your own vegetables, pricking out seeds, or planting splendid roses. Go to a theme park and scream and wave your hands as you plummet down the roller-coaster slide. Buy an ice cream with chocolate sprinkles. Go camping for the weekend and get back to nature. Relish a cold glass of home-made lemonade as you dangle your feet in the pool. Pack up a picnic and head to an empty field where you can spread your lunch on a gingham tablecloth on the fresh grass and breathe the warm air and pick hedgerow berries for dessert.

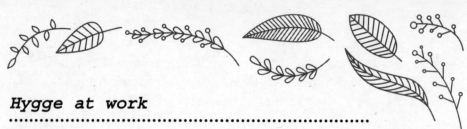

Hygge at work

That feeling of teamwork and joint responsibility can also pervade your workplace if you follow the principles of hygge. Be conscious of your own value and contribution to the business but be aware, also, that others have their role to play and that you all bring different skills, temperaments, strengths, and weaknesses. Try to focus on what you are doing at any given time, rather than always chasing down the next job. Work hard while you are in the office, but maintain your work-life balance. Everyone needs to work late some nights, but don't make it such a habit that neither you nor anyone else remembers what time you are supposed to finish. Try to take a lunch break, preferably away from the office, and enjoy a brief respite from the pressure of work.

Another trap that many of us fall into—but which we should avoid if we are aiming for hygge—is bringing work home with us, either in a briefcase or on our smartphone. Once the working day is over, the work emails should wait their turn until the following morning when you are back in the office. If you keep your phone by your plate at the supper table and deal with endless emails, you are likely to spoil the carefully constructed atmosphere of hygge. No amount of calming incense aroma or flickering candles will divert your attention from the flashing screen and harsh, insistent beep of a smartphone.

The season of good hygge

Christmas exemplifies the spirit of hygge and it is a high point in the year for the Danes. In Denmark, the days are short and darkness comes early, but the glimmer of candlelight can be seen casting its hygge light everywhere: in houses, on the rooftop, and cascading across the streets. Thoughtful gifts, delightful decorations, comforting food, and family togetherness are all contributors to the feeling of cheerful companionship.

Why not introduce some Scandinavian customs to add hygge to your Christmas celebrations? Make an advent wreath with four candles and light one on each Sunday running up to Christmas. Score the numbers 1 to 24 down the side of a tall candle, starting with 1 at the top. At breakfast, light the candle and take it in turns to blow it out when it has burned down to the next date. Include some national flags in your Christmas tree decorations and top it with a star. On one day, why not serve a traditionally Danish dish to bring an extra shot of festive hygge?

Hygge puzzles

There is something very satisfying about solving a puzzle or a conundrum and when the topic and style of the puzzles is hygge, it's a double whammy of feel-good factor. Whether you prefer visual puzzles like matching pairs, mazes, jigsaws, and spot the difference, or whether word puzzles like wordsearches, arrowords, codewords, and word wheels are your choice, there is plenty here to keep you comfortably occupied on your own for an hour or two, or to bring out your sociable side as you divide into teams for a good-natured contest.

You may be familiar with the puzzle styles, or you may want to run through the simple explanatory text that accompanies each one so that you know exactly what to do. Either way, the puzzles will be fun for both beginners and more experienced solvers.

The themes of the puzzles all relate to making you feel hygge because they feature those things we know will bring us that feeling of happiness and contentment. From puzzles set around a comfortable home where you enjoy poetry and books, crafts, and conversation to creative activities such as cooking and sociable times based around games and parties, you'll find hygge on every page. There are puzzles based outdoors, too, bringing the beauty of nature into your view.

Bring more hygge into your life

With all these hygge activities, plus the people and places around us, we can't fail to increase our hygge score and really start to understand this simple but profound concept. Live your life to the full, enjoy the smallest things as much as the big ones, stay calm and balanced, and you really will have discovered the secret of hygge.

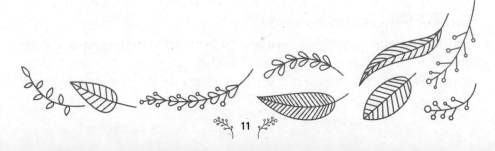

Wordsearch: HAPPY

Can you find all of the listed words hidden in the grid?
They may run forward or backward, in either a
horizontal, vertical or diagonal direction.

```
E E D J C I T A T S C E E D D
C S Q X N E D A Y G Z A T A E
X U W E J N E I K K P Y T L L
Y N N U U M U N Z L R B E G B
L N M C B A P G C U U E O E U
L Y O X J U H L N U R C P L O
O J P P Y Y O U E I P Y K L R
J M P D I K R Y E A L B O Y T
O O R N E D I P A E S I E Q N
V S Y A Z L C M V N T E M A U
I I C F D E L I G H T E D S T
A A F N U I L I C O N T E N T
L W L A Q L A Y R D E T A L E
N S M E R R Y N E H T I L B E
G N I H G U A L T M T N A B E
```

BLITHE	JOCUND	PERKY
BUOYANT	JOLLY	PLEASED
CONTENT	JOVIAL	RADIANT
DELIGHTED	JOYFUL	SMILING
ECSTATIC	LAUGHING	SUNNY
ELATED	LIVELY	THRILLED
EUPHORIC	LUCKY	UNTROUBLED
GLAD	MERRY	UPBEAT

The words are provided, but can you fit them all in the grid?

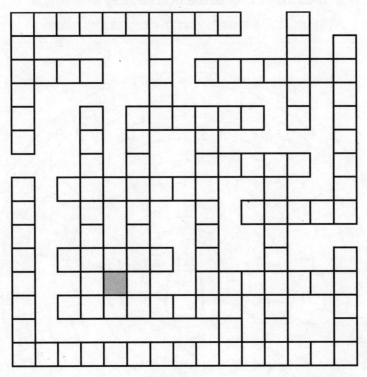

4 letters
IRIS
LILY

5 letters
ASTER
DAISY
LILAC
LUPIN
TANSY
TULIP

6 letters
CROCUS
SALVIA

7 letters
GENTIAN
NIGELLA
PETUNIA

8 letters
LAVENDER
SNOWDROP
XANTHIUM

9 letters
AQUILEGIA
CALENDULA
CELANDINE
COLUMBINE

10 letters
SNAPDRAGON

15 letters
MICHAELMAS
DAISY

Cocoa Mug Maze

Discover a path through the maze to find your prize,
a delicious mug of cocoa overflowing with hygge!

Start at the entrance at the top of the maze.

"Success is peace of mind, which is a
direct result of self satisfaction in
knowing you made the effort to become
the best of which you are capable."

John Wooden

Place all twelve of the pieces into the grid. Any may be rotated or flipped over, but none may touch another, not even diagonally.

The numbers outside the grid refer to the number of consecutive black squares; and each block is separated from the others by at least one white square. For instance, '3 2' could refer to a row with none, one or more white squares, then three black squares, then at least one white square, then two more black squares, followed by any number of white squares.

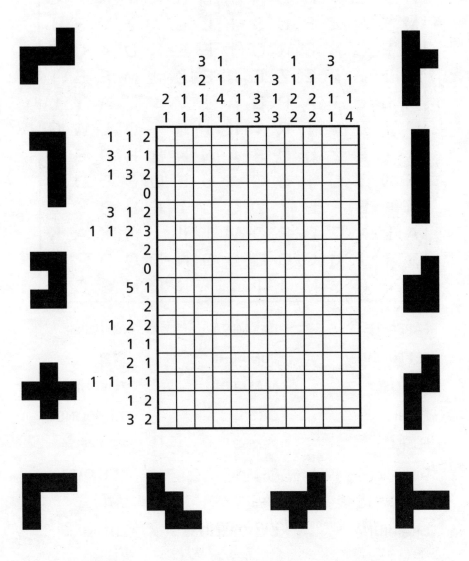

5 Wordsearch: PASTA

Can you find all of the listed words hidden in the grid?
They may run forward or backward, in either a
horizontal, vertical or diagonal direction.

```
E A U E J O X S B L E M M I X
H B A X I S U L L I P Z L U Z
C T U F F O L I G K I G I R W
A E E T R E N I L O P I R T G
M K N Z F U S I L L I J M R I
U F O N E R O I F E R D A U Q
L I E F E Z E P E Z J M F E I
A L L T A P D A L V I T A Y L
S I L Y T R I K I G T O L W G
A I E Z U U F A N K R R D B I
G N T Q I G C A U B O C E D G
N I S P D T Z C L T F H B K Z
A L X G O R O V I L I I X A K
V I I H C C O N G N E O D P P
P F C Y M J I T I K E M S G Y
```

FARFALLE	LASAGNA	ROTINI
FETTUCCINE	LUMACHE	STELLE
FIDEOS	MAFALDE	TORCHIO
FILINI	ORZO	TRIPOLINE
FUSILLI	PENNE	TROFIE
GIGLI	PILLUS	TUFFOLI
GNOCCHI	PIPE	ZITI
GRAMIGNA	QUADREFIORE	ZITONI

The words are provided, but can you fit them all in the grid?

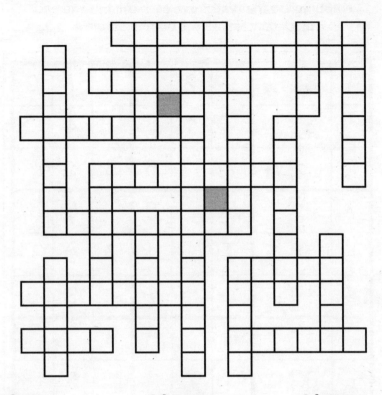

4 letters
PINE
ROSE

5 letters
BASIL
ELEMI
MANGO
MYRRH
PEONY
THYME

6 letters
ALMOND
GINGER
MIMOSA
NUTMEG

7 letters
BAY LEAF
FREESIA

8 letters
BLUEBELL
CARDAMOM
GERANIUM
MARJORAM
ROSEMARY

9 letters
AMBERGRIS
LEMON BALM

13 letters
SAMARKAND
MUSK

Place one of the numbers from 1 to 9 into every empty cell so that each row, each column and each 3x3 block contains all the numbers from 1 to 9.

1	8			2			7	9
	3			1			4	
		9	7		6	3		
7	2		5		9		6	1
		5	4		1	7		
4	1		2		7		3	5
		1	6		5	8		
	6			7			5	
8	5			4			9	7

"Learn to enjoy every minute of your life. Be happy now. Don't wait for something outside of yourself to make you happy in the future. Think how really precious is the time you have to spend, whether it's at work or with your family. Every minute should be enjoyed and savored."

Earl Nightingale

First solve the clues. All of the solutions end with the letter in the middle of the circle, and in every word an additional letter is in place. When the puzzle is complete, reading clockwise around the shaded ring of letters will reveal a word appropriate to the theme of this book.

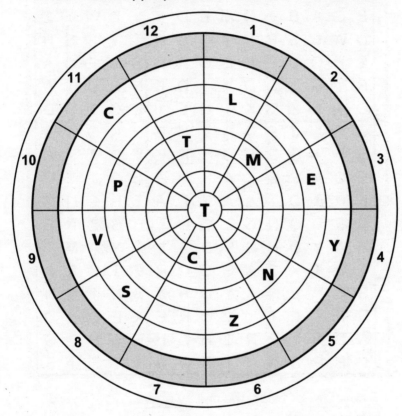

1 Forgiving under provocation

2 Item used as a decoration

3 Largest of its kind

4 Vision

5 Most slender

6 Filbert

7 Precisely and clearly expressed

8 Someone who lives at a particular place

9 Writer of story books

10 Indian or African animal

11 Austrian composer of the *Trout Quintet*

12 Less lengthy route to a destination

Answer: _____

Poetry Wordsearch:
LOVELIEST OF TREES

Can you find all of the underlined words from the poem *Loveliest of Trees* by A. E. Housman hidden in the grid? They may run forward or backward, in either a horizontal, vertical or diagonal direction.

```
Y T N E V E S W W W W F E O N
B G A B T O M L O Y Y D W I Z
D W L G R S T O B N I Y S E H
E H O O E B E O R R S G F G A
R I G Y O D V I D F N H U I W
O T L K M K I N L I E O T O D
C E L J P O A T H E B K O I W
S F I G P L O T R E V D A I W
E O W P D K A R H E L O T T U
E R I O T A A T E A T H L U G
R F O Q N G Z Q N L B S Z P S
H W Y D H D K D J L T Y A M T
T B T X S A S C O R E T C E A
S E R E N A Y O H J S N I N N
N F I F T Y M O R E X E O L D
W O N Y R R E H C U P W H L S
L E P S G N I R P S Y T F I F
```

Loveliest of trees, the <u>cherry now</u>
Is hung <u>with bloom</u> along <u>the bough</u>,
And <u>stands</u> about the <u>woodland ride</u>
Wearing <u>white for Eastertide</u>.
Now, of my <u>threescore</u> years <u>and ten</u>,
<u>Twenty</u> will not come again,
And <u>take from seventy</u> springs <u>a score</u>,
It only leaves me <u>fifty more</u>.
And since to <u>look at things in</u> bloom
<u>Fifty springs</u> are <u>little room</u>,
About the <u>woodlands I will go</u>
To see the cherry hung <u>with snow</u>.

The words are provided, but can you fit them all in the grid?

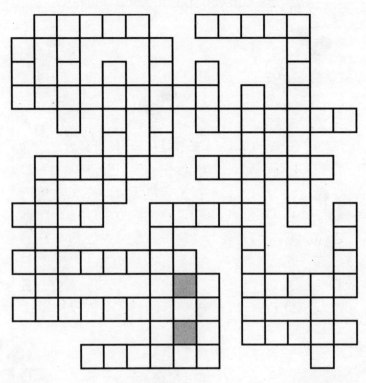

3 letters
JAR
POT

4 letters
BREW
JAVA
MILL
NOIR

5 letters
AROMA
BEANS
HOUSE
IRISH
LATTE
MOCHA
TABLE
WHITE

6 letters
FILTER
GROUND
KENYAN

7 letters
BARISTA
INSTANT
TURKISH

8 letters
ESPRESSO

9 letters
AMERICANO
MACCHIATO
RISTRETTO

11 letters
FRENCH ROAST

Spot the Difference

One of these ice cream treats is different from
the rest. Can you spot the odd one out?

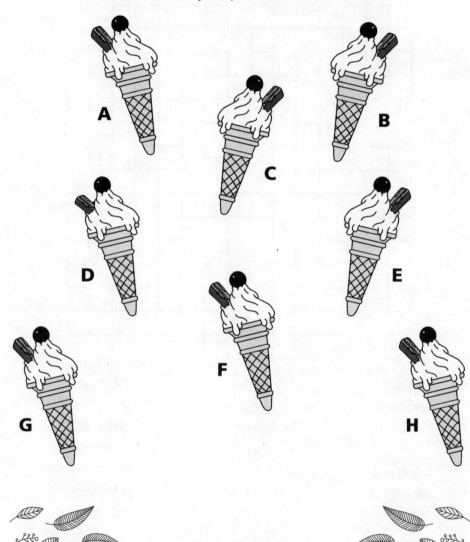

A

B

C

D

E

F

G

H

"The best and most beautiful things in
the world cannot be seen or even touched
- they must be felt with the heart."

Helen Keller

Every clue in this puzzle is an anagram leading to a single-word solution. Correctly solve the anagram on each level of the pyramid and another word will appear, reading down the central column of bricks.

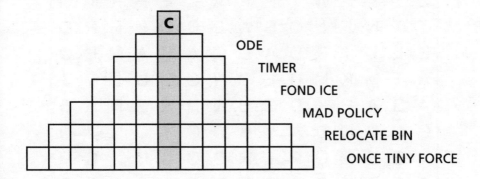

ODE

TIMER

FOND ICE

MAD POLICY

RELOCATE BIN

ONCE TINY FORCE

Using the letters in the Wordwheel, you have ten minutes to find as many words as possible of three letters or more, none of which may be plurals, foreign words or proper nouns. Each word must contain the central letter and no letters can be used more than once per word unless they appear in different spokes of the wheel. There is at least one nine-letter word to be found.

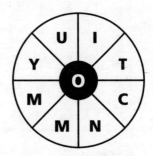

Nine-letter word(s):

_____

"Joy in looking and comprehending is nature's most beautiful gift."

Albert Einstein

Wordsearch: DANCES

Can you find all of the listed words hidden in the grid?
They may run forward or backward, in either a
horizontal, vertical or diagonal direction.

```
Z T L A W I P F A L E E R M O
T T N F L O B W L B O L E R O
E L L I R D A U Q A M A M B O
A T M K M U L G N G M U L V J
A B A P K D G U N N H E R A B
O G V O B W Y B D O Y O N J O
V Z E M G P I R D G C H X C P
D G P J R J P E Y G A C O Q O
T S I W T F S T A Y X K V P I
M V P U I A T T E C A B M A S
E Q N I K F E I W U B P A I G
S V R L M L K J K X N C M I P
N J O M E U A L X Z D I J G M
C P H V N F H N T H S V M C Y
R O G N A T S H I M M Y X V N
```

BOLERO	JITTERBUG	RUMBA
BOP	JIVE	SAMBA
BUNNY HOP	LIMBO	SHAKE
CONGA	MAMBO	SHIMMY
FLAMENCO	MINUET	TANGO
FRUG	POLKA	TWIST
HORNPIPE	QUADRILLE	VELETA
JIG	REEL	WALTZ

Arroword

15

Enter the answer to each clue, one letter per square, in the direction indicated by the arrows. When completed, rearrange the letters in the shaded squares to spell out a word appropriate to the theme of this book.

Size of paper / Spanish sport	▼	In accompaniment or as a companion	▼	Salty Greek cheese	▼	Cone-bearing tree	▼	External forms
◣			▒	▼				
Chief impact of a specified action		Through-out a period of time, poetically	►			Remain, sit tight		Preten-tious
◣					Health resort near a spring / Highway	► ▼		▼
Decorative tie		Stocking support / Ballroom dance	►		▼		▒	
◣	▒	▼	Small case into which an object fits	Hop-drying building / Make unhappy	►			
Narrative poem of popular origin	Put to the test ►		▼	▼			One who looks after a sick relative	
◣						Ooze	▼	Cautious
Slept lightly	Diminutive of Edward ► / Lubricate	►			Watched ►	▼		▼
◣	▼				Epoch ►			
Foreign		Decorative layer ►	▒					
◣				Enquire in a meddle-some way ►				

25

Ladle the letters from the soup tureen and fit one into each of the 26 bowls on the table below, so that the finished result is a complete crossword containing English words. All of the letters in the tureen must be used – thus no letter is used more than once. When rearranged, the letters in the filled bowls spell out a variety of pea.

ABCDEFGHIJK
LMNOPQRS
TUVWXYZ

"Nothing is more beautiful than the loveliness of the woods before sunrise."
George Washington Carver

Which four shapes (two black and two white) can be fitted together to form the dolphin shown here? The pieces may be rotated, but not flipped over.

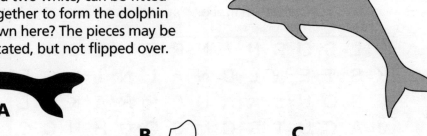

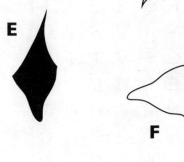

A

B

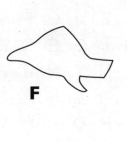

C

D

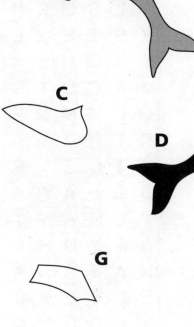

E

F

G

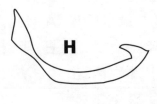

H

I

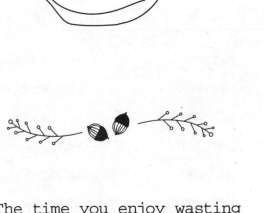

J

"The time you enjoy wasting is not wasting time."

John Lennon

Can you find all of the listed words hidden in the grid?
They may run forward or backward, in either a
horizontal, vertical or diagonal direction.

```
O L S O G N I N R E H Q S I Y
K S T E W L D N A L N I F G E
F B O U S K A G E R R A K R L
J A C U T R O M S O U H H O C
O L K M N E N N A N K A O B R
R T H J M A O K R R S E L I I
D I O S V R R M F V I V S V C
S C L A W A I E A G F V T I C
V S M A M T D L G E D H E S I
A E Y N R S B N T N R F B R T
N A E A W A V A A K A E R H C
E D V E R C X R O L H V O F R
Y A D D V M J V U P P S A L A
H E K R S G N I K I V A E T H
N H E L S I N K I M P J L Y S
```

ARCTIC CIRCLE   HELSINKI   STAVANGER

BALTIC SEA   HERNING   STOCKHOLM

DENMARK   HOLSTEBRO   SVALBARD

FINLAND   LAPLAND   SWEDEN

FJORDS   NARVIK   TROMSO

GLAMA RIVER   NORWAY   UPPSALA

HARDFISKUR   OSLO   VIBORG

HAVARTI   SKAGERRAK   VIKINGS

The words are provided, but can you fit them all in the grid?

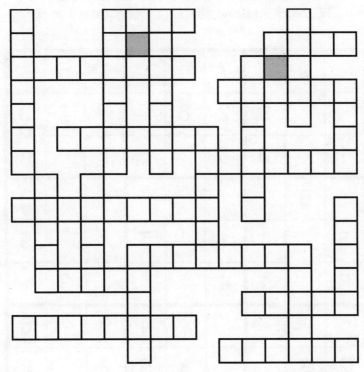

4 letters	**6 letters**	**8 letters**
EGGS	GRATER	CURRANTS
SALT	RECIPE	DECORATE
TRAY	SPONGE	SULTANAS

5 letters	**7 letters**	**9 letters**
CAKES	BEATING	PARCHMENT
CREAM	FILLING	
FLOUR	LOAF TIN	
FRUIT	RAISINS	
ICING	SPATULA	
MIXER	TESTING	
SPOON		
SUGAR		

Sudoku

Place one of the numbers from 1 to 9 into every empty cell so that each row, each column and each 3x3 block contains all the numbers from 1 to 9.

	2		7			1	5	
		9	2	6			7	3
1		3	5					
	6				9	4		8
5			1		7			9
8		1	4				3	
					4	9		6
2	8			3	5	7		
	4	7			2		8	

"Perfect happiness is a beautiful sunset, the giggle of a grandchild, the first snowfall. It's the little things that make happy moments, not the grand events. Joy comes in sips, not gulps."

Sharon Draper

Discover a path through the maze to find the
knitting, and relax by making a scarf!

Start at the entrance at the top of the maze.

"The happiness of your life depends upon
the quality of your thoughts: therefore,
guard accordingly, and take care that
you entertain no notions unsuitable
to virtue and reasonable nature."

Marcus Aurelius

Wordsearch: BREAKFAST

Can you find all of the listed words hidden in the grid? They may run forward or backward, in either a horizontal, vertical or diagonal direction.

```
M F Y Z G S E K A C N A P R A
P U Z T M S O T I P M M F E A
Z S E O T A M O T I A S T T S
W J V S T P L L C R L F O R N
A O Z M L T A H M A O E A U A
F R E G V I S A E T E U S G E
F A E G I B L R O F M Y T O B
L N A E O A E P F N D Z N Y G
E G M D D C L O P U A X A H O
S E U E C O C B A G E L S O V
Q J F L Y N M J O I R S S N Q
A U F I Q G J S M E B P I E T
H I I O A P R I C O T S O Y H
E C N B T I U R F E P A R G A
Z E S S A U S A G E S A C G M
```

APRICOTS   CROISSANTS   ORANGE JUICE

BACON   GRAPEFRUIT   PANCAKES

BAGELS   HAM   POT OF TEA

BEANS   HONEY   SAUSAGES

BOILED EGG   MARMALADE   TOAST

BREAD   MUESLI   TOMATOES

CEREALS   MUFFINS   WAFFLES

COFFEE   OATMEAL   YOGURT

The words are provided, but can you fit them all in the grid?

3 letters
MAY

4 letters
BUDS
EGGS
LENT
LILY

5 letters
BUNNY
FRESH
GREEN
GUSTY

LAMBS
MARCH
NESTS

6 letters
CALVES
GROWTH
SHOOTS
SPRING
TULIPS

7 letters
ANEMONE
PUDDLES
RAINBOW
SHOWERS

8 letters
SNOWDROP

9 letters
NARCISSUS

13 letters
MORRIS DANCERS

Place all twelve of the pieces into the grid. Any may be rotated or flipped over, but none may touch another, not even diagonally.

The numbers outside the grid refer to the number of consecutive black squares; and each block is separated from the others by at least one white square. For instance, '3 2' could refer to a row with none, one or more white squares, then three black squares, then at least one white square, then two more black squares, followed by any number of white squares.

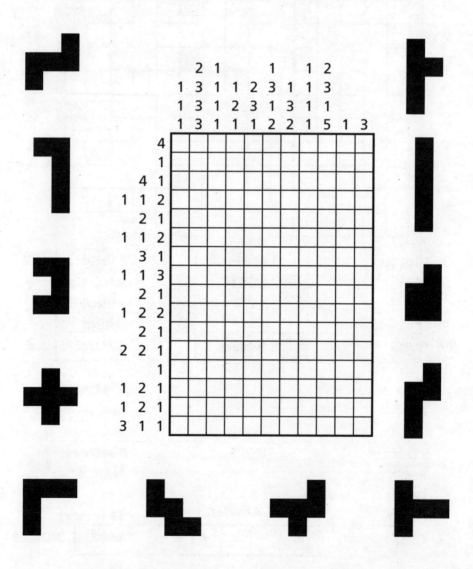

Every letter in this crossword has been replaced by a number,
the number remaining the same for that letter wherever it occurs.
Can you substitute numbers for letters and complete the crossword?

Some letters have already been entered into the
grid, to help you on your way. When finished, use
the code to spell out the name of a butterfly.

	1	2	3	4	5	6	7	8	9	10	11	12	13
		N		**D**			**E**						
	14	15	16	17	18	19	20	21	22	23	24	25	26

Grid (rows A–M):

A	21	14	15	11	2	1		7		10		4
B	4		24			19	21	9	7 E	2 N	4 D	7	17
C	8	21	25	16		22		21		21		14
D	12		2	12	25	16		10	11	1	2	21	19
E	10			14		7		11				4
F	18	21	14	23	24		16	22	12	5	12	7	18
G		13		19		18		2		12		2
H	21	13	13	7	21	17	10		4	21	17	18	10
I		7				21		2		17			22
J	7	2	1	12	19	6		22	21	18	15		19
K		4		2		6		18		20	22	2	7
L	3	11	19	4	19	11	6	7			22		25
M		26		22		14		4	7	21	4	7	2

Side labels: A B C D E F G H I J K L M (left) · N O P Q R S T U V W X Y Z (right)

Answer

10	3	21	19	19	22	3	18	21	11	19

Wordsearch: GOOD-LOOKING

Can you find all of the listed words hidden in the grid?
They may run forward or backward, in either a
horizontal, vertical or diagonal direction.

```
D Y N K J Y N N O B P H R F E
S E Z S U O R O M A L G S E M
K Q F E T N A I D A R H B T O
E X C O M E L Y D W N Z T C S
G X J R Z A L S M A R T N H N
C R Q Y C N T B V F P Q A I I
L O A U S F H J A X G P G N W
I U R N I Y V S H N E L E G V
E Z F Y D S D U I L O Y L R F
I N E I T Q I N Y L O S E E U
B F I T T N T A S Y V R H P
R N A F U U E F E D T T E E R
D E V I T C A R T T A C S L P
V S V S R T N E P M F D N F Y
A L L U R I N G B F O X U V R
```

ALLURING	ELEGANT	PERSONABLE
ATTRACTIVE	EXQUISITE	PRETTY
BEAUTIFUL	FAIR	RADIANT
BONNY	FETCHING	SHAPELY
COMELY	FINE	SMART
CUTE	GLAMOROUS	STUNNING
DANDY	GRAND	STYLISH
DAPPER	LOVELY	WINSOME

The words are provided, but can you fit them all in the grid?

3 letters
COB
RYE

4 letters
NAAN
OVEN
SALT

5 letters
BAGEL
BAKER
BOARD
BROWN
DOUGH

FLOUR
KNEAD
SAUCE
STICK
TOAST
WHEAT
WHITE

6 letters
CRUMBS
FRENCH
GARLIC
MILLER
RISING

7 letters
BRIOCHE
CROUTON

8 letters
CHAPATTI

9 letters
WHOLEMEAL

First solve the clues. All of the solutions end with the letter in the middle of the circle, and in every word an additional letter is in place. When the puzzle is complete, reading clockwise around the shaded ring of letters will reveal the names of two birds.

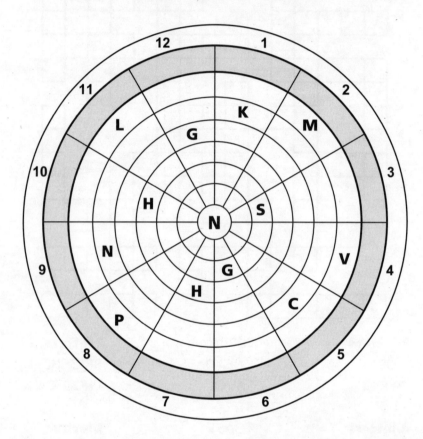

1 Country, capital Islamabad
2 Jail
3 Male child of one's child
4 Action by a landlord that compels a tenant to leave the premises
5 Event
6 Gas that forms approximately 78% of Earth's atmosphere

7 Surname of brothers George and Ira, of musical fame
8 Worker who makes glasses for remedying defects of vision
9 Charitable gift
10 Security guard
11 Conjuring trick
12 Metallic element used to make light-bulb filaments

Answer: _____ **and** _____

Place the answers in order across the horizontal rows. When completed correctly, reading down each of the shaded columns will reveal the name of a plant.

1. Collarbone
2. Put up with
3. Amulet, charm
4. Shiitake, for example
5. Government representative abroad
6. Former British coin worth five new pence
7. Patron saint of children
8. Unnecessary

"Be happy with what you have and what you are, be generous with both, and you won't have to hunt for happiness."

William E. Gladstone

Can you find all of the listed words hidden in the grid?
They may run forward or backward, in either a
horizontal, vertical or diagonal direction.

```
K F T N R F H C D E D V D D W
X F S H W F L A S H F R Y S E
M A A C O R D S T A E H E R S
A P O A D O Z S L Q C G N Z U
E D T O E L Q E J B L B C H O
T T N P V S R R N Z O K V N S
S H A L I O B O S I M M E R P
K S L N L E J L B F C I C L E
B I L E I N U E V O L Y G K L
R N Z S S R N C D A B A A D W
O R G I M G A D E R S B M Y S
I A R A O G L M O B I A K B T
L G I R K E B W C C R Q U P E
Q A L B E D N N S W E A T T W
I W L H B E K F B I M P B D E
```

BAKE	DEVIL	SAUTE
BARBECUE	FLAMBE	SIMMER
BOIL	FLASH FRY	SMOKE
BRAISE	GARNISH	SOUSE
BROIL	GRILL	STEAM
BROWN	MARINATE	STEW
CASSEROLE	POACH	SWEAT
CODDLE	REHEAT	TOAST

The words are provided, but can you fit them all in the grid?

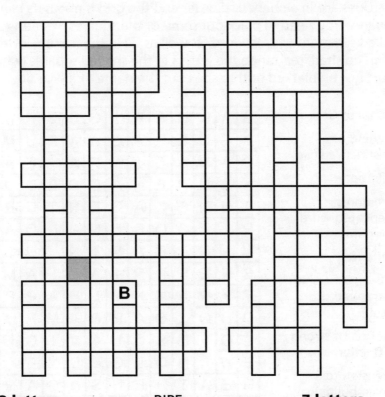

3 letters
RYE

4 letters
BALE
BARN
BEET
CART
CROP
FARM
HOPS
HUSK
LOAF
MILL
REAP

RIPE
SACK
SILO

5 letters
FEAST
FIELD
FRUIT
TITHE

6 letters
APPLES
BARLEY
BINDER
SUPPER

7 letters
BERRIES
FLOWERS

8 letters
CHERRIES
FESTIVAL
TEAMWORK
THRESHER

10 letters
VEGETABLES

Straightforward clues are presented with the crossword grid but the clues are in alphabetical order and the grid is minus its black squares. You need to black out some of the squares, resulting in a filled symmetrical crossword, as well as fill in the missing letters. When finished, rearrange the letters in the shaded squares (which must not be blacked out) to spell out the name of a wild flower.

B	A	N	D	E	R	I	G	O	U	R	E	D
A	G	U	E	S	A	G	A	W	P	U	M	O
C	A	V	A	L	I		R	A		E	A	L
K		N	R	E	N	A	D	D	E	D	D	L
A	N	N	E		A	C	E	N	T	U	R	Y
R	I	P	S	O	B	E	N	D	E	D	A	R
M		N	T	R	A	S	I	N		U	S	E
S	N	E	E	R	R	I	A	L	L	A	M	A
T	Y	R	A	N	N	Y	L	H	A	P	P	Y
O	H	O		S	A	P	B	A	M	P	O	E
L	O	V	E	S	C	L	A	V	I	C	L	E
E	W	A	N	O	L	O		D	N	E		T
N	E	A	T	H	E	N	S	A	G	A	R	B

Capital of Greece

Clothing of a distinctive style

Collarbone

Commonly repeated word or phrase

Contented

Criticising harshly on a web site (coll)

Emotion of strong affection

Extension to a main building

Former name of the Indian city of Chennai

Haphazardly, at random

Heating elements in an electric fire

Marine crustacean

Most expensive

Quality of being extremely careful and thorough

Royalist supporter of Charles I

One more time

Oppression

Period of 100 years

Relating to Antarctic or Arctic regions

Representative

Secure against leakage

Shrub with large fragrant tubular white or yellow flowers

Stripe of a contrasting shade

Steep in a liquid

Thrown into a state of disarray

Water falling in drops

Fit the listed words into the grid below (one letter is already in place), then rearrange the letters in the shaded squares to form the name of a flower.

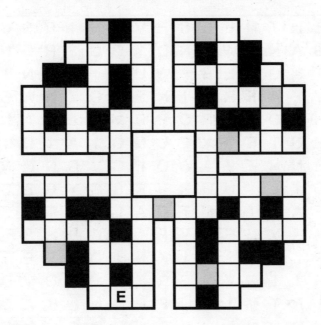

3 letters	**4 letters**		**5 letters**	
AGO	ABUT	KNOT	AMAZE	LIMBO
BUT	AURA	LASS	CLERK	LUSTY
DUO	BAKE	MAUL	FLASK	RANCH
HID	BLED	ODDS	FROTH	SHARK
KEG	DANK	RAKE	KHAKI	THIEF
NIL	GOOD	TAXI	LATIN	TOPIC
OAF				
TEN				

"We usually find that it is the simplest things – not the greatest occasions – that in retrospect give off the greatest glow of happiness."

Bob Hope

Can you find all of the lines from the poem *Beauty* by John Masefield hidden in the grid? They may run forward or backward, in either a horizontal, vertical or diagonal direction.

```
E H T N E E S E V A H I B S G
G A N D W I N D Y G G S R Q N
T R G K E B F W U N I O I N I
V F A F R A I N P I O Z N W G
H H O S X R Q B R M U L G A N
H G T S S X E U N O I A I D I
E N N E E A W O L C V D N N R
O I L I U H N U R S S Y G E B
F A T T G M T D A L R A T E S
S R Y E E N Y F I L A P H S L
P L V R S H I K N I O R E E I
A I I G V N E R E H M I D V D
I R T M I S U F P M N L K A O
N P R U L U S S U S O G Q H F
P A F O N P H M D D E Q E I F
W U W E M E R A A N I H X H A
S N M E L O S N I S A O T A D
```

I have seen dawn

And sunset

On moors

And windy

Hills, coming

In solemn

Beauty

Like slow

Old

Tunes

Of Spain.

I have seen the

Lady April

Bringing the

Daffodils, bringing

The springing

Grass and

The soft

Warm

April rain.

The words are provided, but can you fit them all in the grid?

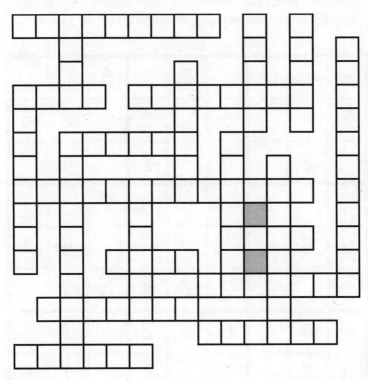

4 letters
DICE
LUDO
POOL
SNAP

5 letters
CHESS
FIVES

6 letters
AIKIDO
BO-PEEP
BRIDGE

PELOTA
SEVENS

7 letters
CANASTA
MAH-JONG
MARBLES

8 letters
CHECKERS
PING-PONG
SCRABBLE

9 letters
BILLIARDS

10 letters
BASKETBALL

11 letters
TABLE TENNIS

13 letters
POSTMAN'S
KNOCK

Place one of the numbers from 1 to 9 into every
empty cell so that each row, each column and each
3x3 block contains all the numbers from 1 to 9.

		1		2		5		
9	4		5		3		2	6
	2		9		7		4	
		3	8	6	9	2		
2	6						8	7
		9	2	7	4	3		
	1		6		2		7	
3	9		7		8		1	5
		7		9		4		

"Most people don't allow
the happy moment, because
they're so busy trying
to get a happy life."

Esther Hicks

Place the listed words horizontally into the grid, so that when read from top left to bottom right, the letters in the shaded squares spell out the name of a spice. Some letters are already in place.

ALKANET

BUGBANE

CATMINT

FLYTRAP

LUCERNE

NIGELLA

SAFFRON

		T			
			R		
		G			
			R		

"Courtesies of a small and trivial character are the ones which strike deepest in the grateful and appreciating heart."

Henry Clay

Can you find all of the listed words hidden in the grid?
They may run forward or backward, in either a
horizontal, vertical or diagonal direction.

```
D K A T L P M L R U G U G D X
R P Y E E I E I G N N D D X J
I B Q L H A A T F O T W N F C
B P P Y G R R T R O O S T E R
E N K L Y W O L N E I S N X J
T V E E S H Q E J I L P E B V
A W O F X M E B N F P I P I T
G H U D B X X U I V D F J Q F
I S T O R K T N Y X E E A Z W
R E I N G H C T B E N G U L L
F J P S A H K I T E K I R H S
W V H T K W U N X I R R B E F
M Y C V C I S G A O X P U O T
T H R U S H N N O E G I P T R
Y D H U R X H K P X N X J O R
```

DOVE	LITTLE BUNTING	ROOK
EAGLE	NUTHATCH	ROOSTER
EGRET	PETREL	SHRIKE
FINCH	PIGEON	SISKIN
FRIGATE BIRD	PINTAIL	STORK
GOOSE	PIPIT	SWAN
GULL	RHEA	THRUSH
KITE	ROBIN	TURKEY

The words are provided, but can you fit them all in the grid?

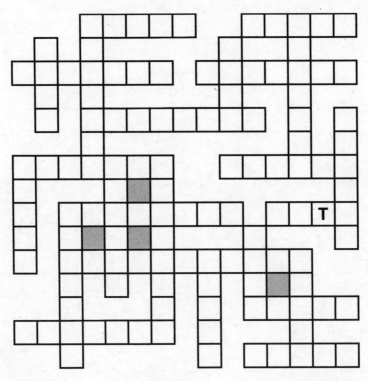

4 letters
CAKE
DATE
FOOD
HATS

5 letters
CARDS
DANCE
GAMES
GIFTS
MUSIC
SONGS
THEME

6 letters
GUESTS
SPEECH
WISHES

7 letters
BANNERS
CANDLES
FRIENDS
GLASSES
INDOORS
MARQUEE
NAPKINS

8 letters
ICE CREAM
LAUGHTER
SURPRISE

11 letters
DECORATIONS

Candlelit Maze

Discover a path through the maze to reach the light!
Start at the entrance at the top of the maze.

"The moments of happiness we enjoy take us by surprise. It is not that we seize them, but that they seize us."

Ashley Montagu

Place all twelve of the pieces into the grid. Any may be rotated or flipped over, but none may touch another, not even diagonally.

The numbers outside the grid refer to the number of consecutive black squares; and each block is separated from the others by at least one white square. For instance, '3 2' could refer to a row with none, one or more white squares, then three black squares, then at least one white square, then two more black squares, followed by any number of white squares.

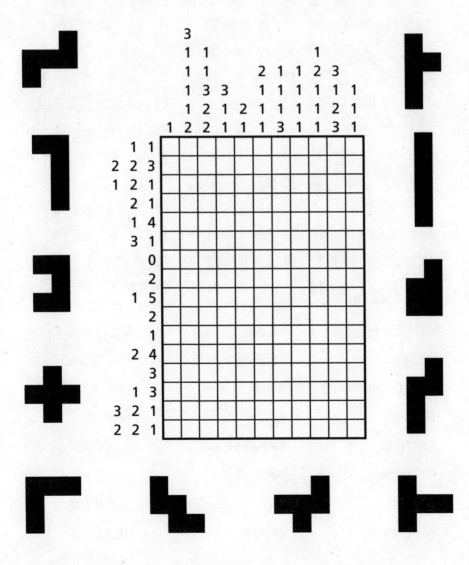

Wordsearch: FLOWERS

Can you find all of the listed words hidden in the grid?
They may run forward or backward, in either a
horizontal, vertical or diagonal direction.

```
C J B I B R E V A P A P N R N
A C C H J W Y E I S A L V I A
L H A S H A S Q S O V T A G Y
I Z P N Q H I G I N L S J S A
L R T O T P A N R L T E N F N
H S F W P E D Y I E S A T V T
F S I D J P R L R X T J I V I
R J R R B H Y B A S O U A E R
P A H O X L I P U F C L X R R
N P T P N O G L X R K S G B H
W O I O A X U G Y P Y C G E I
X N D Y A M E E I Y M B J N N
K I O W I S M L H N E G E A U
C C V M U R U W M P G A H L M
M A G E N T I A N R Q D L P L
```

ANTIRRHINUM	LILAC	SALVIA
ASTER	LILY	SNOWDROP
CANTERBURY BELL	MIMULUS	STOCK
DAISY	OXLIP	TANSY
GENTIAN	PAPAVER	THRIFT
GLOXINIA	PHLOX	TULIP
IRIS	PINK	VERBENA
JAPONICA	POPPY	VIOLET

The words are provided, but can you fit them all in the grid?

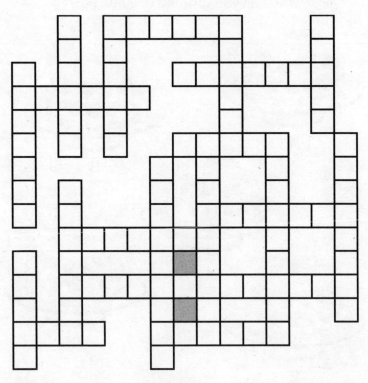

4 letters
MUSK

5 letters
AROMA
ROSES
SCENT

6 letters
CITRUS
FLORAL
FRUITY
LILIES
ORCHID
SPICES

7 letters
BOUQUET
COLOGNE
INCENSE
OAKMOSS
VIOLETS

8 letters
LAVENDER

9 letters
ORRIS ROOT
REDOLENCE
SWEETNESS

13 letters
EAU-DE-TOILETTE

One of these fruity desserts is different from the rest. Can you spot the odd one out?

A

B

C

D

E

F

G

"Laughter is an instant vacation."

Milton Berle

Can you find all of the listed words hidden in the grid?
They may run forward or backward, in either a
horizontal, vertical or diagonal direction.

```
Y Q I B K D P T E N E S S A M
S H L D S C H E R U B I N I K
S P L Z C S H O A A C G X O C
U U E M W P U A T E Z I B L U
B R I T T E N A N S C O K L L
E C H R U D O R R D L L M A G
D E C W N E V O H T E E B V M
G L N W G Y R I L N S L D A X
O L O F F E N B A C H E S C R
U Q P V N I Z S P U C C I N I
N I D G D J S M E T A N A O V
O C A O M H X E T G M X G E Z
D W R J I T T O N E M S R L H
R O N A D R O I G M M D L Q W
B E R L I O Z S X Q I U E L Z
```

BEETHOVEN	GLUCK	OFFENBACH
BERLIOZ	GOUNOD	PONCHIELLI
BIZET	HANDEL	PUCCINI
BORODIN	LEONCAVALLO	PURCELL
BRITTEN	MASCAGNI	SMETANA
CHERUBINI	MASSENET	STRAUSS
DEBUSSY	MENOTTI	VERDI
GIORDANO	MOZART	WAGNER

First solve the clues. All of the solutions end with the letter in the middle of the circle, and in every word an additional letter is in place. When the puzzle is complete, reading clockwise around the shaded ring of letters will reveal the names of two birds.

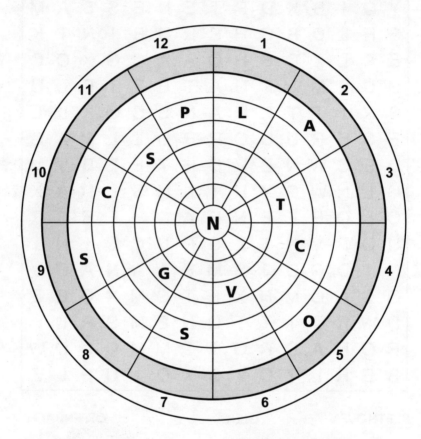

1 Male shop assistant

2 Temple to all the gods

3 Cherished desire

4 Response

5 Native of Bucharest, for example

6 State of being disregarded or forgotten

7 Receptacle for rubbish

8 Faith

9 Hired murderer

10 Holiday

11 Albert ___, physicist (1879–1955)

12 ___ Bonaparte, emperor of the French (1769–1821)

Answer: _____ **and** _____

Which four shapes (two black and two white) can be fitted together to form the tree shown here? The pieces may be rotated, but not flipped over.

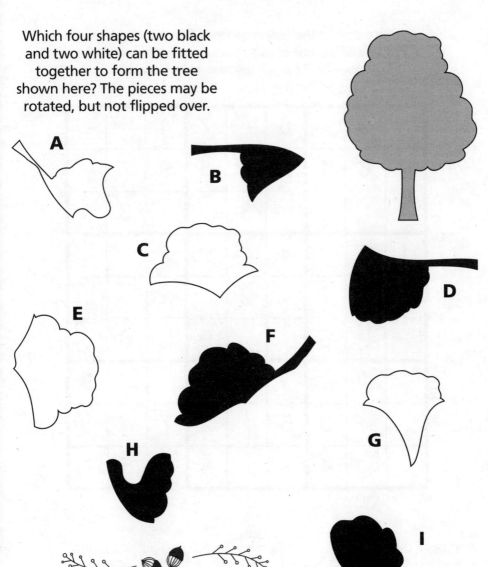

"I don't have to chase extraordinary moments to find happiness – it's right in front of me if I'm paying attention and practicing gratitude."

Brené Brown

Place one of the numbers from 1 to 9 into every
empty cell so that each row, each column and each
3x3 block contains all the numbers from 1 to 9.

	9		6		7	4		
	6	1	2		5	9		
4				3			8	
1	3		4			2		
		7		2		1		
		8			9		6	5
	1			7				9
		3	5		2	7	4	
		4	1		8		5	

"Laughter is the sun
that drives winter from
the human face."

Victor Hugo

Can you find all of the listed words hidden in the grid?
They may run forward or backward, in either a
horizontal, vertical or diagonal direction.

```
S S D L L F C H T D K W C T G
T Z P W J C E D G R A E G D R
N D R O T I U R F T A R N M T
A C T B N T K B E N M Y I R E
R L F E Y G R R U A E X L A M
R H U A Q E E D E T E A L G P
U B U T C N S R B R T S I U E
C P P I A H C A O P N E F S R
V K P N S P W X N I T E R W A
P E S G X P S B S A R D N W T
U S N P S I O I R U T E T B U
O V E N C R A O R U O L F H R
U X U I R R C O N E M I U P E
K I N G R E D I E N T S N S M
S G G E D V Z Q K Y J F X F X
```

BEATING	FLOUR	SPATULA
BOWL	FRUIT	SPONGE
BUTTER	ICING	SPOON
CREAM	INGREDIENTS	SUGAR
CURRANTS	MIXER	SULTANAS
DECORATE	OVEN	TEMPERATURE
EGGS	RAISINS	TRAY
FILLING	RECIPE	WATER

The words are provided, but can you fit them all in the grid?

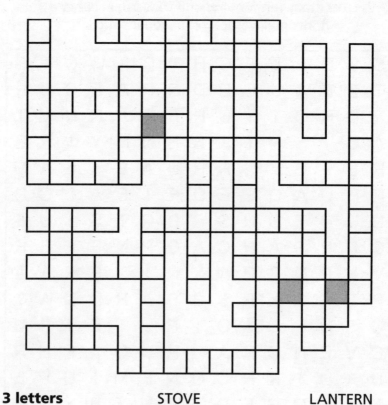

3 letters	STOVE	LANTERN
AXE	TORCH	OPEN AIR

4 letters	**6 letters**	**8 letters**
PEGS	ESCAPE	OUTDOORS
RAIN	FLY NET	ROOF RACK
SITE	KETTLE	
TENT	STAKES	**11 letters**
WOOD		COUNTRY CODE

	7 letters	GROUNDSHEET
5 letters	CANTEEN	
BEACH	CUTLERY	
GUIDE	GRIDDLE	
POLES	HATCHET	

Only two of sunshades are identical in every way. Can you spot the matching pair? They are mirror images of each other.

52   Pyragram

Every clue in this puzzle is an anagram leading to a single-word solution. Correctly solve the anagram on each level of the pyramid and another word will appear, reading down the central column of bricks.

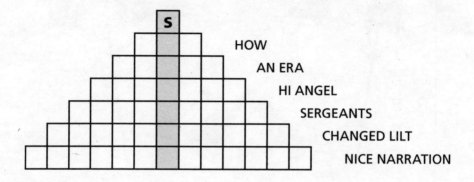

HOW

AN ERA

HI ANGEL

SERGEANTS

CHANGED LILT

NICE NARRATION

53   Word Wheel

Using the letters in the Wordwheel, you have ten minutes to find as many words as possible of three letters or more, none of which may be plurals, foreign words or proper nouns. Each word must contain the central letter and no letters can be used more than once per word unless they appear in different spokes of the wheel. There is at least one nine-letter word to be found.

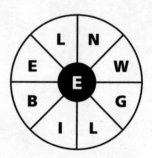

Nine-letter word(s):

_____

"If you surrendered to the air, you could ride it."

Toni Morrison

Can you find all of the listed words hidden in the grid?
They may run forward or backward, in either a
horizontal, vertical or diagonal direction.

```
D K O W F X Y H I F L B L D Q
S I S P A O T B X E C A E N T
Z T C E J S K B S I W D D U R
D A A A N O H A U L E D O O E
R B I T R I E S E E M R M R B
A P Q W U E L I F R G Q H G L
W J C Z Q E P I G T A A P E I
I G M O T L L M E H C H H R F
N B R P L L A T E T L E Z O S
G F M B L L E R U T C I P F E
K R N I V J A S U C R H C S Z
X E T W M V R G S M D A I L A
O S V T S E K T E W M O K N L
S C H O O L S V U E E F O B G
O O R E P A P R O F I L E W V
```

ASPECT	FOREGROUND	PROFILE
BATIK	FRESCO	RELIEF
CAMEO	GLAZE	SCHOOL
COLLAGE	LINES	STATUE
DRAWING	MODEL	STILL LIFE
EASEL	MURAL	TEMPERA
ETCHING	PAPER	WASH
FILBERT	PICTURE	WOODCUT

The words are provided, but can you fit them all in the grid?

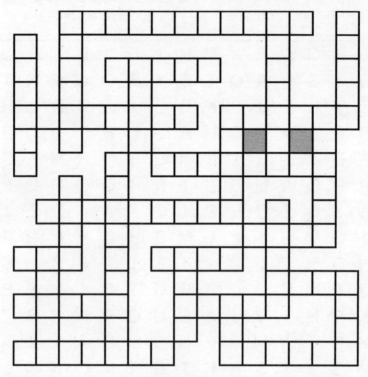

3 letters	**5 letters**	**7 letters**
MAY	APRIL	ANEMONE
SUN	BUNNY	BLOSSOM
	FRESH	
4 letters	GRASS	**8 letters**
BUDS	GREEN	BLUEBELL
EGGS	GUSTY	CLEANING
LENT	MARCH	
LILY		**9 letters**
NEST	**6 letters**	MIGRATION
RAIN	CALVES	NARCISSUS
TIDE	CROCUS	
	GROWTH	**11 letters**
	NATURE	CATERPILLAR
	TULIPS	

Patchwork Quilt

Place all twelve of the pieces into the grid. Any may be rotated or flipped over, but none may touch another, not even diagonally.

The numbers outside the grid refer to the number of consecutive black squares; and each block is separated from the others by at least one white square. For instance, '3 2' could refer to a row with none, one or more white squares, then three black squares, then at least one white square, then two more black squares, followed by any number of white squares.

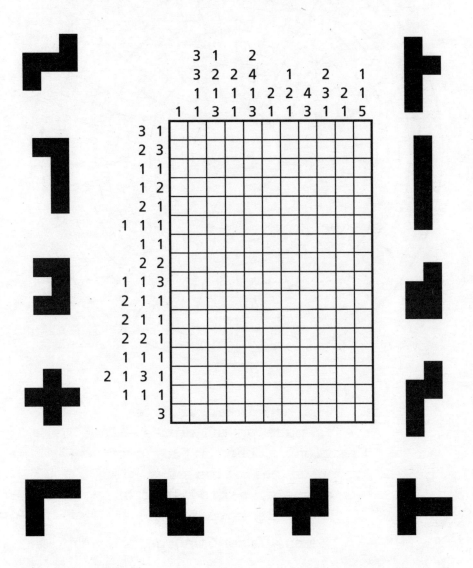

Cherry Pie Maze

Discover a path through the maze to find your prize, a warm slice of cherry pie!

Start at the entrance at the top of the maze.

"The happiness of life
Is made up of minute
Fractions – the little, soon
Forgotten charities of a kiss
Or a smile, a kind look or
Heartfelt compliment."

Samuel Taylor Coleridge

Wordsearch: INDOOR GAMES

58

Can you find all of the listed words hidden in the grid?
They may run forward or backward, in either a
horizontal, vertical or diagonal direction.

```
G W R S K N I W Y L D D I T S
G W M S T X B D X R I U C E G
N M K R E R C A N A S T A L U
O A K G I L A T M H E V N D Y
J C R D M Q B D P E L O T A G
H H G M M W L R Z E Y U S R B
A E E S W O S K A Q G Y O C O
M C D O G R N E Y M P U L S P
A K R O T O E O V P L I I T E
I E J X M C X S P E S M T A E
K R T A E I A C T O N I A C P
I S T M C G N T H L L S I Y O
D V U I L K E O C E I Y R W O
O P M Q S K S S E I S N E S L
P J S E V I F U M S T S G J E
```

AIKIDO	DARTS	OLD MAID
ARM WRESTLING	DOMINOES	PELOTA
BO-PEEP	FIVES	POOL
BRIDGE	I SPY	ROULETTE
CANASTA	JACKS	SEVENS
CAT'S CRADLE	MAH-JONGG	SOLITAIRE
CHECKERS	MARBLES	TIC TAC TOE
CHESS	MONOPOLY	TIDDLYWINKS

67

The words are provided, but can you fit them all in the grid?

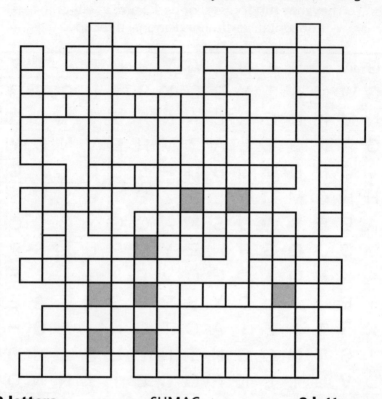

3 letters
IVY

4 letters
DILL
ILEX
TAGS
WREN

5 letters
AGAVE
GORSE
LILAC
MOWER
SALIX

SUMAC
THUJA
TRAYS
VIOLA

6 letters
ACACIA
BARROW
DAHLIA
WEEVIL

7 letters
RAGWORT
TRELLIS

8 letters
ASPHODEL
GLOXINIA

9 letters
BUTTERFLY
DRAGONFLY
FLOWERPOT

10 letters
MARGUERITE

Arroword

60

Enter the answer to each clue, one letter per square, in the direction indicated by the arrows. When completed, rearrange the letters in the shaded squares to spell out a word appropriate to the theme of this book.

Pioneering motor manufacturer (5,4)	Go by	Notorious Roman emperor	▼	Minimum to maintain a nuclear reaction (8,4)	▼	Young newts	▼	Reach a destination
◣	▼	▼						
Hawaiian garland of flowers ▶				Unwell		That is to say (2,3)		Tea container
Aesthetic ▶				▼		▼		▼
◣					Egg cells ▶			
Destroy or ruin	Scratched at, as if with talons ▶							
◣			Intent	Ambit		Penetrate gradually		
Queen of the gods in Greek mythology	Tight	Finally ▶	▼	▼		▼		
◣	▼					Long-tailed rodent		Bruce ___, former expert kung fu actor
Nuclear	Not concerned with right or wrong ▶					▼		▼
◣			Speed ▶					
Creeping or crawling invertebrates	Be in an agitated emotional state ▶							

69

Can you find all of the listed words hidden in the grid?
They may run forward or backward, in either a
horizontal, vertical or diagonal direction.

```
E S C R V A C N K F C B E D C
R N E P Q A N E M O N E L A X
L O L T I L V A S C F I L X A
L S A E H L P F O Y D I S E U
E M N L H I S L R O L U U V R
B A D O Z C T W F W C P A O I
E R I I W S D F O O Q I E L C
U A N V F D A Q R C L Q I G U
L H E O M D R C P L W R N X L
B W O C Z R X O E T A P S O A
Z T Y S N A P M P C I I B F L
F R E E S I A A S L R M T S L
N U I B L C L U U I Y L I L I
D F T O N E M T E G R O F E U
A S U E L K N I W I R E P A M
```

ALLIUM	CROCUS	MUSCARI
ANEMONE	DAFFODIL	PANSY
AURICULA	FORGET-ME-NOT	PERIWINKLE
BLUEBELL	FOXGLOVE	RAMSONS
CAMELLIA	FREESIA	SCILLA
CELANDINE	IRIS	SNOWDROP
COLTSFOOT	LILAC	TULIP
COWSLIP	LILY	VIOLET

Place one of the numbers from 1 to 9 into every
empty cell so that each row, each column and each
3x3 block contains all the numbers from 1 to 9.

	4			6	2			7
		7	5			3		2
9	1				4	8		
7	6	8		4	3			
5								1
			9	8		7	3	6
		4	3				9	8
8		6			1	2		
1			2	9			5	

"Contentment is natural
wealth, luxury is
artificial poverty."

Socrates

First solve the clues. All of the solutions end with the letter in the middle of the circle, and in every word an additional letter is in place. When the puzzle is complete, reading clockwise around the shaded ring of letters will reveal a popular outdoor pastime.

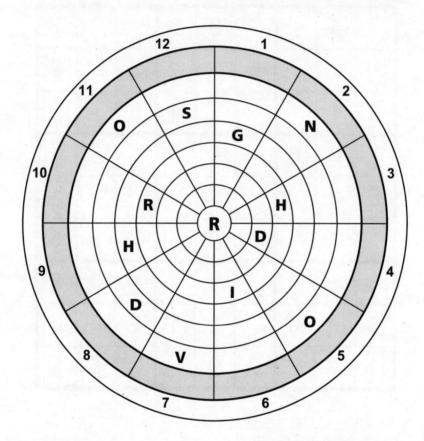

1 More lustrous

2 Designer of machinery

3 Large comfortable seat

4 Record of annual dates

5 Person who owns a guest house

6 Passageway

7 Eavesdrop

8 Person who acts as a link between parties

9 Unmarried man

10 Of the middle of a region or country

11 Month with 30 days

12 Filaments from a web spun by a spider

Answer: _____

Can you find all of the underlined words from the poem *The Rainbow* by Christina Rossetti hidden in the grid? They may run forward or backward, in either a horizontal, vertical or diagonal direction.

```
E H T N O N O A O K L W M L B
E C E E G R B E K B N P O I P
A N D S H I P S U M S F R A G
J M Z E A Z R I S E Q Q F S U
L X J H W E L R E O S B D T O
U Y S T H D L R T R A U A A E
Y D E N S H T P Y A I C O H W
R D G A L E Y D L U L V R T Y
E P D H H J N I C O O A E T P
I E I T V E A H U S N T T R N
T V R V V S N D P M S E L W S
T H B A S N S O F A R G X O E
E V E T E T T V A P F V K B K
R H A S B R Y K S E H T V E O
P O I T E N E A Q M L V R H R
B Y P V U A P H N W W Z B T X
T Z O G Y K S O T H T R A E F
```

Boats <u>sail</u> on the <u>rivers</u>,

And ships <u>sail on the</u> seas;

But <u>clouds</u> that <u>sail</u> across <u>the sky</u>

Are <u>prettier</u> than these.

<u>There are</u> <u>bridges</u> <u>on the</u> rivers,

<u>As pretty</u> as you <u>please</u>;

But <u>the bow</u> that <u>bridges</u> heaven,

And <u>overtops</u> <u>the trees</u>,

And <u>builds</u> a <u>road from</u> <u>earth to sky</u>,

Is prettier far <u>than these</u>.

The words are provided, but can you fit them all in the grid?

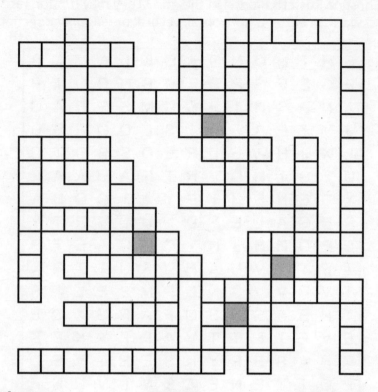

3 letters
TOM

4 letters
CUTE
MANX
PAWS
TAIL

5 letters
CLAWS
FELIX
FLEAS
HAIRS

MOUSE
QUEEN

6 letters
BASKET
CATNIP
COLLAR
GINGER
NEPETA

7 letters
CATFLAP
FUR BALL
MOGGIES
SINGING

8 letters
FOOD BOWL
GARFIELD

9 letters
MARMALADE
NINE LIVES

Which four shapes (two black and two white) can be fitted together to form the seahorse shown here? The pieces may be rotated, but not flipped over.

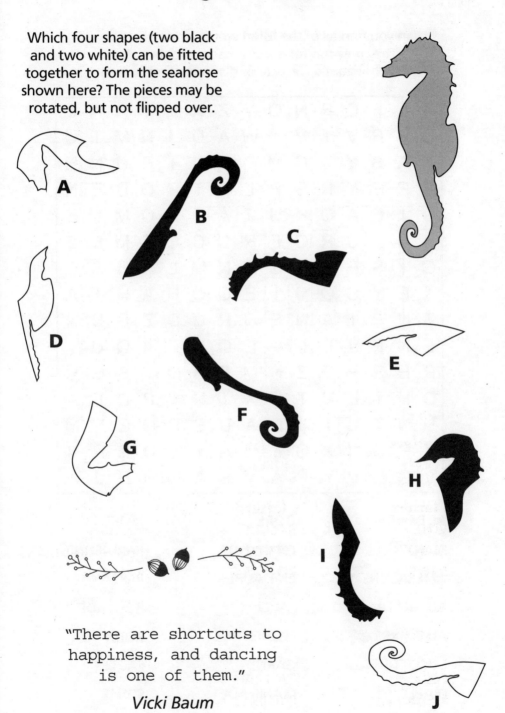

A

B

C

D

E

F

G

H

I

"There are shortcuts to happiness, and dancing is one of them."

Vicki Baum

J

Wordsearch: COOKERY TERMS

Can you find all of the listed words hidden in the grid?
They may run forward or backward, in either a
horizontal, vertical or diagonal direction.

```
A L F O R N O Y Z X E Y R A E
C P R V I V I W A D J N M T U
X A B Y J C M Q A N I E U N H
C R G Y R S P L D T R O D E N
O I E A O K U Z A I R O M L E
C S F U R O F R C C G F M B E
O I S P R N G A N M L A U A D
T E Y O O U I E O O H A H I A
T N R I A N E Q R C D Z S D N
E N F V E L T E O N F A Q U I
R E R R E Z N M E B Q I B G R
O H I E V T E X T N V P D F A
U N T L I J D A U S S O O V M
X P S N X G L N A Y Y D R R V
V G E V Y P A Y S A N N E J W
```

AL DENTE	DORE	MORNAY
AL FORNO	EN CROUTE	PARISIENNE
AMERICAINE	EN DAUBE	PAYSANNE
AU GRATIN	FARCI	ROULADE
AU POIVRE	FLORENTINE	ROUX
COCOTTE	GARNI	SAUTE
DIABLE	MARINADE	SOUSE
DOPIAZA	MOCHA	STIR-FRY

The words are provided, but can you fit them all in the grid?

4 letters
BOWL
BUNS
CAKE
MUGS
PATE
SALT
WINE

5 letters
APPLE
CLOTH
FLASK
PLATE

SALAD
WATER

6 letters
BANANA
CHEESE
COFFEE
CRISPS
GATEAU
PEPPER
SWEETS

7 letters
CHICKEN
LETTUCE
PICKLES

8 letters
HAM ROLLS
LEMONADE

10 letters
MAYONNAISE

Discover a path through the maze to find the knitting,
and unwind by making a lovely warm blanket!

Start at the entrance at the top of the maze.

"The power of finding beauty in
the humblest of things makes
home happy and life lovely."

Louisa May Alcott

Place all twelve of the pieces into the grid. Any may be rotated or flipped over, but none may touch another, not even diagonally.

The numbers outside the grid refer to the number of consecutive black squares; and each block is separated from the others by at least one white square. For instance, '3 2' could refer to a row with none, one or more white squares, then three black squares, then at least one white square, then two more black squares, followed by any number of white squares.

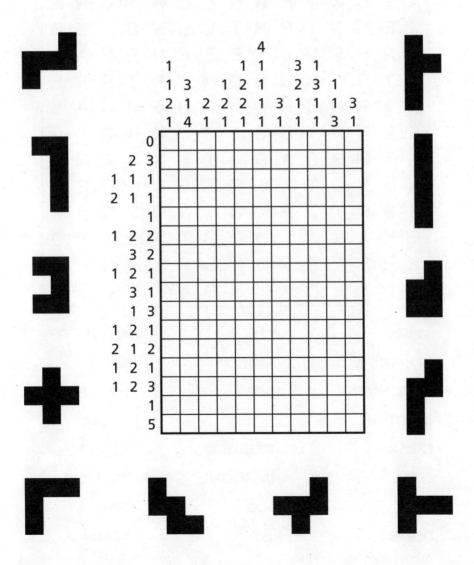

Wordsearch: LOVING WORDS

Can you find all of the listed words hidden in the grid?
They may run forward or backward, in either a
horizontal, vertical or diagonal direction.

```
E  T  I  D  O  R  H  P  A  T  R  A  G  U  S
O  T  H  Q  C  T  A  Y  G  T  E  Q  I  H  A
H  W  B  E  A  U  T  I  F  U  L  N  L  C  F
A  Y  D  X  M  K  R  N  E  O  W  T  D  R  X
J  E  H  S  I  R  H  I  V  U  N  B  I  E  D
I  N  H  S  U  L  T  E  E  E  R  E  E  A  R
J  T  S  W  U  U  R  O  M  I  N  T  R  F  E
D  I  P  U  C  R  W  H  F  D  E  H  U  A  E
E  E  X  H  T  D  C  I  S  O  K  A  S  I  R
A  T  M  S  O  A  Q  H  T  L  X  N  A  R  I
N  D  N  O  T  K  I  T  T  E  N  D  E  E  S
G  D  R  T  T  P  K  N  T  N  O  S  R  S  E
E  K  A  K  W  I  D  O  G  T  V  O  T  T  D
L  H  E  Y  B  P  O  M  E  X  S  M  Q  H  U
I  L  Y  L  O  V  I  N  G  A  A  E  L  Z  Q
```

ANGEL	DOTE	KITTEN
APHRODITE	EMOTION	LOVER
ATTACHMENT	EROS	LOVING
BEAUTIFUL	FAIREST	SUGAR
CRUSH	FRIENDSHIP	TENDER
CUPID	HANDSOME	TREASURE
CUTIE	IDOL	TRUE
DESIRE	KISS	YEARN

Place one of the numbers from 1 to 9 into every
empty cell so that each row, each column and each
3x3 block contains all the numbers from 1 to 9.

7					8			
6				2		4	8	9
1			4	3				
	6	4	8		3	1	2	
8		9				3		5
	7	1	5		2	6	9	
				5	4			1
9	5	6		7				4
			6					2

"Think big thoughts but
relish small pleasures."

H. Jackson Brown, Jr.

Spot the Difference

One of these dolls is different from the rest.
Can you spot the odd one out?

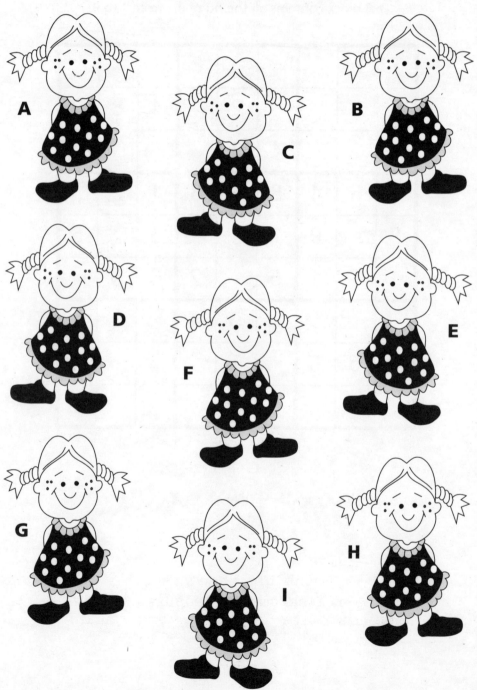

Ladle the letters from the soup tureen and fit one into each of the 26 bowls on the table below, so that the finished result is a complete crossword containing English words. All of the letters in the tureen must be used – thus no letter is used more than once. When rearranged, the letters in the filled bowls spell out a variety of peach.

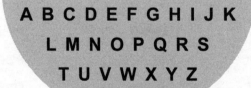

A B C D E F G H I J K

L M N O P Q R S

T U V W X Y Z

"I grew up around people that enjoyed life day to day and found pleasure in simple things."

Josh Turner

Wordsearch: WOOD TYPES

Can you find all of the listed words hidden in the grid?
They may run forward or backward, in either a
horizontal, vertical or diagonal direction.

```
R S P D W O L Z F H G Q K Y I
L V E T O I W I C K E R F P M
E A W G H L R P R E D L A M L
L E O P V S I W E Y S O U V E
D A J Y E E U V Q T Y S B X H
K A D M N D E T E K H D Y C O
A B L Z E K O J P D Y V R B V
I C E L O E B O N Y V A E R S
T H K N I N Y J W J L L I I P
G E T E Z D A C S E Y A W A R
H S A U L E A K H V L O C R U
P T V T N P Q N T L L P R U C
Q N X I E L A R A L P O P P E
G U P A L A A M I R A S L A B
C T Y G J L K W W P G I G K A
```

ALDER	ELM	PINE
APPLEWOOD	EUCALYPTUS	POPLAR
ASH	FIR	SPRUCE
BALSA	GRANADILLA	TEAK
BRIAR	LARCH	WALNUT
CHESTNUT	MAPLE	WICKER
DEAL	OAK	WILLOW
EBONY	OLIVE	YEW

The words are provided, but can you fit them all in the grid?

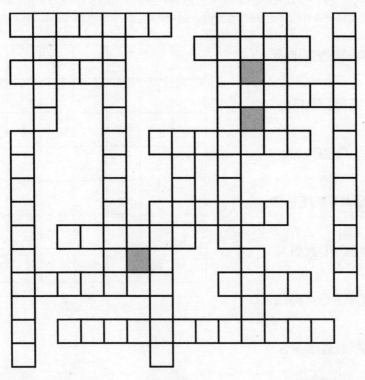

4 letters
KIWI
LIME

5 letters
HONEY
LEMON
MANGO
PEACH

6 letters
CHERRY
COFFEE
PEANUT
TOFFEE

7 letters
APRICOT
CARAMEL
PRALINE
SHERBET

10 letters
CAPPUCCINO
REDCURRANT

12 letters
CLOTTED
   CREAM
FOREST FRUITS
RUM AND
   RAISIN

Place the listed words horizontally into the grid, so that when read from top left to bottom right, the letters in the shaded squares spell out the name of a vegetable. Some letters are already in place.

ANEMONE

CHERVIL

LOBELIA

MAYWEED

MORINGA

OREGANO

RHUBARB

"Simplicity is the ultimate sophistication."

Leonardo da Vinci

First solve the clues. All of the solutions end with the letter in the middle of the circle, and in every word an additional letter is in place. When the puzzle is complete, reading clockwise around the shaded ring of letters will reveal a word appropriate to the theme of this book.

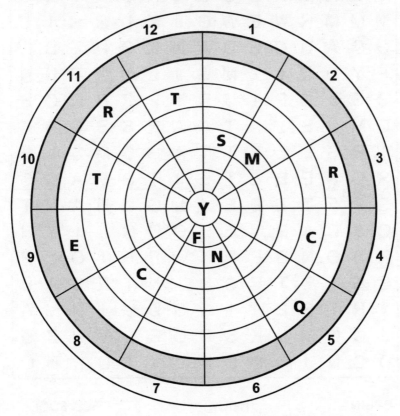

1 Lineage

2 Apothecary's shop

3 Main concern, precedence

4 Process of getting better

5 Fairness, parity

6 Legal tender of a country

7 Distinguish

8 Done in a friendly spirit

9 Characteristic likelihood of or natural disposition toward

10 Close or warm friendship

11 Commonplace

12 Event celebrated at Christmas

Answer: _____

Can you find all of the listed words hidden in the grid?
They may run forward or backward, in either a
horizontal, vertical or diagonal direction.

```
T O R T N Z S Q T A C K I N G
M M M R N E W G J X L R R I L
O O A U C E D W N K O P F B W
F Y D Q A Z M G J L O X P B N
S S L E P T U R I P P B D O B
C M J S L A T A A N S B G B K
I R S L L L T T A G G M S L E
S O S E B E T E J T H E A C G
S F F T L E E J L O U H A N T
O S C A R V I R O D C L I Y H
R S O N B E E K W P E T Q C R
S E T Z T R S D I N T E S A E
Y R T S E W I N G U M I N M A
J D O M L K S C C E L V H Z D
D C N J Q O E R L K T D P H O
```

BOBBIN	HOOKS	SELVEDGE
CHALK	LACE	SEWING
COTTON	MODEL	SILK
CUTTING	NEEDLE	SPOOL
DRESS FORM	PATTERN	TACKING
EDGING	PINS	TAILOR
FABRIC	REELS	THREAD
GARMENT	SCISSORS	YARN

The words are provided, but can you fit them all in the grid?

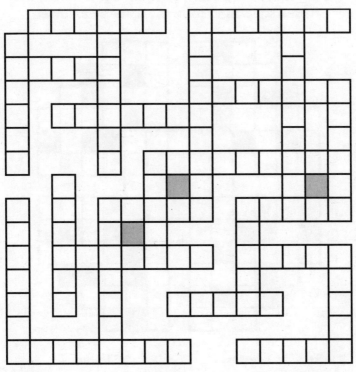

5 letters
BOATS
BRINY
INLET
POOLS
SPADE
SPRAY
TIDES
TOWEL
WAVES

6 letters
BIKINI
LIMPET
SHELLS
SUNBED

7 letters
BATHING
MUSSELS
PARASOL
PEBBLES
SANDALS
SHINGLE
SHRIMPS

8 letters
SOFT SAND

9 letters
BEACH-BALL
LIFEGUARD
PROMENADE

Fit the listed words into the grid below (one letter
is already in place), then rearrange the letters in the
shaded squares to form the name of a flower.

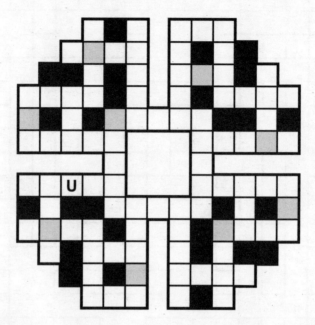

3 letters	4 letters		5 letters	
ERA	BIKE	KEEL	ADULT	NOBLE
GAP	BIND	LOST	AMPLE	NUTTY
LET	CROP	MALT	BATHE	PESTO
MOB	CUSP	PARK	ENTRY	PLANT
NAP	DAIS	RIFT	GHOUL	ROWAN
OAR	DEFY	WEST	NEWTS	SPRAY
WAR				
YET				

"A life-long blessing for children is
to fill them with warm memories of
times together. Happy memories become
treasures in the heart to pull out
on the tough days of adulthood."
Charlotte Kasl

Every letter in this crossword has been replaced by a number,
the number remaining the same for that letter wherever it occurs.
Can you substitute numbers for letters and complete the crossword?

Some letters have already been entered into the
grid, to help you on your way. When finished, use
the code to spell out the name of a butterfly.

A	22	23	15	7	6		10	23	6	23	9	24	19	N
B	19		21		21		7		23		24		14	O
C	19	10	19	1	23	16	20		15	8	7	14	18	P
D	6		1		25		26		21		1		1	Q
E	21	23	7	16		22	23	20		3	5	1	23	R
F			4		17	3	12		1				11	S
G	7	14	4	16	24	13		2	3	10	22	7	19	T
H	14				18		25	7	8		1			U
I	15	19	23	10		6	23	25		18	23	16	19	V
	S	**E**	**A**											
J	25		10		4		1		4		11		11	W
K	19	1	23	15	19		15	23	24	15	23	18	19	X
L	6		2		19		3		15		20		14	Y
M	8	1	19	23	15	3	14		15	6	3	24	8	Z

1	2	3	4	5	6	7	8	9	10	11	12	13
14	15 **S**	16	17	18	19 **E**	20	21	22	23 **A**	24	25	26

Answer

6	23	22	22	23	18	19		26	21	7	8	19

Wordsearch: BOOKS

Can you find all of the listed words hidden in the grid?
They may run forward or backward, in either a
horizontal, vertical or diagonal direction.

```
K W H T Y R J T F I C T I O N
S B D O O D E S I O N X D L J
A V B L U E U T Q T S E A H E
H E J P Q M J T I A L T O M R
E A F C D U R L S R U E O J V
A N T H O L O G Y E W T J R N
Z X H L Y O T R I A I X H V Y
C D R Q A V I L N D Y R W O Z
C F E I X S D B A I X P E A R
U R C Y R T E O P N F G J S Q
B U I N D E X L P G R I R S M
I F P M E M F A D U N U C M G
B Z E J E K V A I K D E O S O
L Z S J S U R U A S E H T J J
E Z O C H R O N I C L E H E L
```

ANTHOLOGY	INDEX	STORY
ATLAS	JOURNAL	STUDY
AUTHOR	PLOT	TEXT
BIBLE	POETRY	THESAURUS
CHRONICLE	READING	TITLE
CRIME	RECIPES	TOME
EDITOR	SCI-FI	VOLUME
FICTION	SERIES	WRITER

The words are provided, but can you fit them all in the grid?

4 letters
GLAD

5 letters
JOLLY
LUCKY
MERRY
PERKY

6 letters
ELATED
JOCUND
JOVIAL
JOYFUL
LIVELY

7 letters
PLEASED

8 letters
ANIMATED
THRILLED

9 letters
EXUBERANT
FORTUNATE
FRIVOLOUS
GRATIFIED
OVERJOYED

10 letters
UNTROUBLED

11 letters
ON CLOUD NINE

Candlelit Maze

Discover a path through the maze to reach the light!
Start at the entrance at the top of the maze.

"Even though I don't have a lot of spare
time, what I do have I'm very protective
of, and so I make sure to have a
normal life and to remember that, while
it's important to keep in mind these
conflicts are ongoing, it's also important
to enjoy simple pleasures, too."

Clarissa Ward

Place one of the numbers from 1 to 9 into every empty cell so that each row, each column and each 3x3 block contains all the numbers from 1 to 9.

		8	3				7	6
		2		5	1	3		8
	9		8					5
6				7		8	1	
	7		6		9		4	
	3	9		4				2
1					7		3	
3		4	9	1		6		
9	5				6	2		

"It's easy to impress me. I don't need a fancy party to be happy. Just good friends, good food, and good laughs. I'm happy. I'm satisfied. I'm content."

Maria Sharapova

The words are provided, but can you fit them all in the grid?

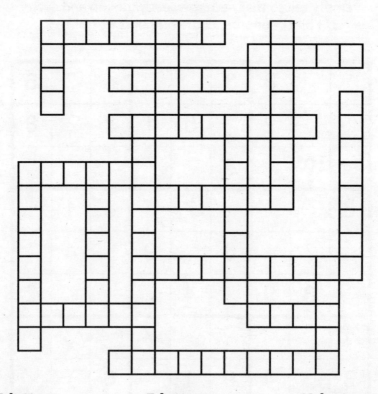

4 letters	**7 letters**	**10 letters**
MANX	BURMESE	ABYSSINIAN
THAI	PERSIAN	TURKISH VAN

5 letters	**8 letters**	**11 letters**
ASIAN	BALINESE	EGYPTIAN MAU
KORAT	BURMILLA	
TABBY	KARELIAN	
	MUNCHKIN	
6 letters	SIBERIAN	
BIRMAN		
BOMBAY	**9 letters**	
LAPERM	PETERBALD	

Place all twelve of the pieces into the grid. Any may be rotated or flipped over, but none may touch another, not even diagonally.

The numbers outside the grid refer to the number of consecutive black squares; and each block is separated from the others by at least one white square. For instance, '3 2' could refer to a row with none, one or more white squares, then three black squares, then at least one white square, then two more black squares, followed by any number of white squares.

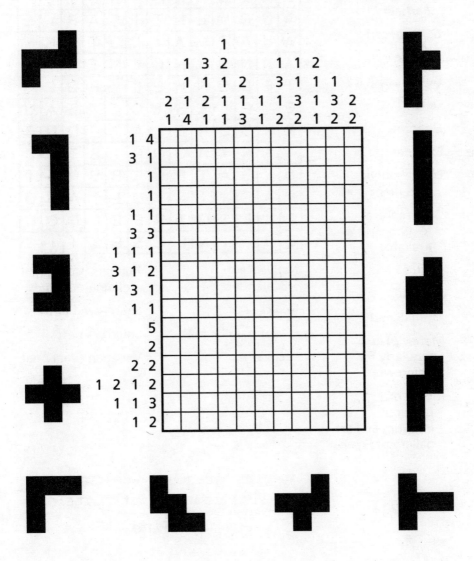

Straightforward clues are presented with the crossword grid but the clues are in alphabetical order and the grid is minus its black squares. You need to black out some of the squares, resulting in a filled symmetrical crossword, as well as fill in the missing letters. When finished, rearrange the letters in the shaded squares (which must not be blacked out) to spell out the name of a wild flower.

Brine

Showing a lack of partiality

Commenced

Cut thinly

Deliciously juicy

Detect

Elaborate cake

Exclude

Formal public statement

Geographical feature such as Krakatoa

Hostile

Increase

Mismatched

Money paid regularly for doing work

Musée du ___, principal museum and art gallery of France

Native New Zealander

Novices

Pair of parallel rails

Peculiar

Runners used for gliding over snow

Sharp-eyed birds

Squirrel's nest

Venetian canal boat

Weeps convulsively

S	O	B		T	U	N	B	I	A	S	E	D
E	W	E	U	R	R	O	U	N	D	T	L	
A	U	G	M	E	N	T	I	C	A	R	V	E
W	S	A	T	M	A	I	L	O	T	A	E	Y
A	N	N	O		N	C	E	M	E	N	T	E
T	E	N	O	N	H	E	L		E	G	E	
E		G	L	E	S	A	G	A	T	E	A	U
R	K	O	O	R	E	L	A	T	E	D	U	S
W	A	N	T	A	G	O	N	I	S	T	I	C
O	L	D	A	T	E	U	R	B	E	R	S	I
M	A	O		I	N	V	O	L	C	A	N	O
I	L	L	S	O	T	R	E	E	L	C	O	U
T	R	A	I	N	E	E	S	E	S		I	S

"The greatest wealth is to live content with little."

Plato

98

Pyragram

Every clue in this puzzle is an anagram leading to a single-word solution. Correctly solve the anagram on each level of the pyramid and another word will appear, reading down the central column of bricks.

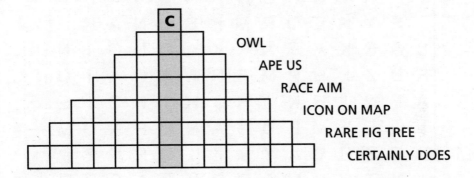

OWL

APE US

RACE AIM

ICON ON MAP

RARE FIG TREE

CERTAINLY DOES

Word Wheel

Using the letters in the Wordwheel, you have ten minutes to find as many words as possible of three letters or more, none of which may be plurals, foreign words or proper nouns. Each word must contain the central letter and no letters can be used more than once per word unless they appear in different spokes of the wheel. There is at least one nine-letter word to be found.

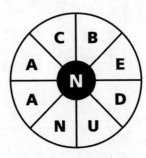

Nine-letter word(s):

_____

"A house is no home unless it contain food and fire for the mind as well as for the body."

Margaret Fuller

Wordsearch:
CLASSICAL MUSIC TITLES

Can you find all of the listed words hidden in the grid?
They may run forward or backward, in either a
horizontal, vertical or diagonal direction.

```
V G A V W R S W A N L A K E F
T S Y K E O R M F S U N A R U
S A R K A P A K K A O U G I U
R U Z L H P M F R W A O A I O
A F N I H N I H J R I H S I E
L O E E M E U G A R P P N O M
O E S U V A Y M Z I G P E Z P
I N T S S M A R P Y S A E D E
P U P G A T Q Y F P F S O L R
A T A V A T L V N F A R E A O
T P R P T A B O R T M C I M R
I E J A Q T R D U I I Y I E L
T N O R G C A R N I V A L R Y
A G M I R I N V Y H G J B B V
N G G S E N C L X O V M H D G
```

AUTUMN	NIMROD	TAMARA
CARNIVAL	PARIS	TAPIOLA
EMPEROR	PRAGUE	TASSO
EN SAGA	SAPPHO	TITAN
LA MER	SARKA	TRAGIC
MARS	SATURN	URANUS
MESSIAH	SWAN LAKE	VENUS
NEPTUNE	TABOR	VLTAVA

The words are provided, but can you fit them all in the grid?

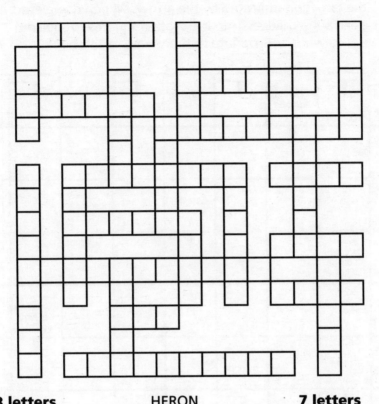

3 letters	HERON	7 letters
AUK	HOBBY	BLUE TIT

4 letters	6 letters	8 letters
CROW	AVOCET	DOTTEREL
GULL	BULBUL	
KITE	CURLEW	9 letters
RHEA	DIPPER	DOWITCHER
ROOK	LINNET	GYRFALCON
SWAN	PLOVER	
	TURKEY	10 letters
		SHEARWATER

5 letters
BOOBY
CRANE
GREBE

11 letters
TREE CREEPER

Enter the answer to each clue, one letter per square, in
the direction indicated by the arrows. When completed,
rearrange the letters in the shaded squares to spell out
a word appropriate to the theme of this book.

Penulti-mate Greek letter	▼	Elaborately adorned	▼	Angler's basket	▼	Unflus-tered	▼	Type of food shop (abbr)
Magician ►		▼						
⌐				Encoun-tered		Digress		Blockade
Calami-tous	Greek goddess of divine retribution ►			▼		▼		▼
Flair ►							Tempera-ture below freezing point	
Region	Cause		Concise in manner ►				▼	
∟	▼		⌐	Off the cuff (2,3)	Abbrevia-tion for a particular month of the year ►			
Round objects used in games		Bait		Change course in sailing ►				
∟		▼			Friend	Massage		Deviate erratically from a set course
Chinese dynasty (AD 581–618) ►				Animal hunted or caught for food ►	▼	▼		▼
Globe ► / A person in general				Halo of light ►				
∟			Hinge joint in the arm ►					

First solve the clues. All of the solutions end with the letter in the middle of the circle, and in every word an additional letter is in place. When the puzzle is complete, reading clockwise around the shaded ring of letters will reveal the names of two birds.

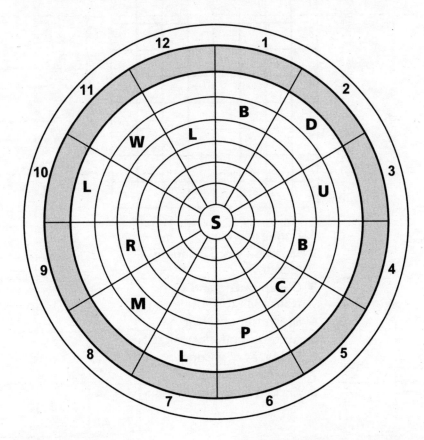

1 Legendary, marvellous
2 State of inactivity
3 Sickening
4 Three-headed dog guarding the entrance to Hades
5 Mythological hero noted for his strength, who performed 12 tasks to gain immortality

6 Cold-blooded vertebrates such as tortoises and snakes
7 Dots in a text showing suppression of words
8 Capital of Syria
9 Armed fighters
10 US Prairie State
11 In these times
12 Young geese

Answer: _____ **and** _____

Columns

Place the answers in order across the horizontal rows. When completed correctly, reading down each of the shaded columns will reveal the name of a plant.

1 Unmarried man
2 Japanese word meaning 'goodbye'
3 Queen of England from 1837 to 1901
4 Spectator, observer
5 Absurd or inferior imitation
6 Folksy, as of wisdom
7 Reverse (a ruling, etc)
8 Ancient language of India

"Hygge is about making the most of what we have in abundance: the everyday."

Meik Wiking

The words are provided, but can you fit them all in the grid?

5 letters
ICING
LARDY
LAYER
MOCHA
POUND

6 letters
CARROT
CHEESE
CHERRY
DUNDEE
ECCLES
MARBLE

ORANGE
SCONES

7 letters
CURRANT
FILLING
MIXTURE

8 letters
DOUGHNUT
MACAROON
MARZIPAN

9 letters
CHRISTMAS

11 letters
LEMON SPONGE

Can you find all of the underlined words from the poem *Leisure* by W. H. Davies hidden in the grid? They may run forward or backward, in either a horizontal, vertical or diagonal direction.

```
N T S S I H T S I T A H W S R
E N R I C H T H A T E Q S Y F
E B S N H C T N G M P Q E T U
S V A B G T R U I I U Z K U S
A V G R C U A T A I L U J A T
E Z R O T V O E R H J Y L E R
R A M A N N N R N T W K A B E
A G G D E I E M H E L O C D A
T Z J G S L I P O F B R O C M
S R A T S F O L L U F N A D S
N O U H P O J F J F T N M C S
C N I F R A E A X G D H Q L T
F D H L L I T T I A W V E J I
E N I S W O C D N A P E E H S
Z F Z G E R A C F O L L U F R
E Q S K F R E H H C T A W P Y
A M E R A T S D N A D N A T S
```

What is this life if, full of care,
We have no time to stand and stare?—
No time to stand beneath the boughs,
And stare as long as sheep and cows:
No time to see, when woods we pass,
Where squirrels hide their nuts in grass:
No time to see, in broad daylight,
Streams full of stars, like skies at night:
No time to turn at Beauty's glance,
And watch her feet, how they can dance:
No time to wait till her mouth can
Enrich that smile her eyes began?
A poor life this if, full of care,
We have no time to stand and stare.

Discover a path through the maze to find your prize,
a delicious mug of cocoa overflowing with hygge!

Start at the entrance at the top of the maze.

"Being solitary is being alone well:
being alone luxuriously immersed in
doings of your own choice, aware of
the fullness of your won presence
rather than of the absence of others.
Because solitude is an achievement."

Alice Koller

Place one of the numbers from 1 to 9 into every
empty cell so that each row, each column and each
3x3 block contains all the numbers from 1 to 9.

	3	2		9		1		7
			5	4	7			
		9					8	6
3	5	8	6				9	
6			7		5			2
	1				9	6	4	5
8	6					2		
			2	7	3			
7		5		6		9	1	

"Be thankful for what
you have; you'll end
up having more. If you
concentrate on what you
don't have, you will never,
ever have enough."

Oprah Winfrey

Can you find all of the listed words hidden in the grid?
They may run forward or backward, in either a
horizontal, vertical or diagonal direction.

```
U P B H T W O R G G G R X P Z
W B R B Y A S V R S X Y Y U V
E O U B J M N E T T E Q K S W
A D B J B E E O H M Q M D S F
S R K N Y N O Y L U U M Z Y Y
J E F I I H N C V E I P S W T
J V J Q S A A E I S N H T I S
M E S D P L R U O B O T L L U
B F F R V D C L L W X A I L G
O S I E A F I O E K M N D O L
H L S N R L S R T B T E O W O
U S T E Y S S B S E W M F P K
V C S Y O Z U T Y G P O F S M
W H A M N I S D Q G U N A O F
M M H N J I N O G S P E D P X
```

ANEMONE	FEVER	MAY
APRIL	FRESH	NARCISSUS
BLOSSOM	GREEN	PUSSY WILLOW
BUDS	GROWTH	RAINBOW
CALVES	GUSTY	SHOOTS
DAFFODIL	LAMBS	SHOWERS
EGGS	LENT	VERDANT
EQUINOX	LILY	VIOLETS

Criss Cross: SOUP

The words are provided, but can you fit them all in the grid?

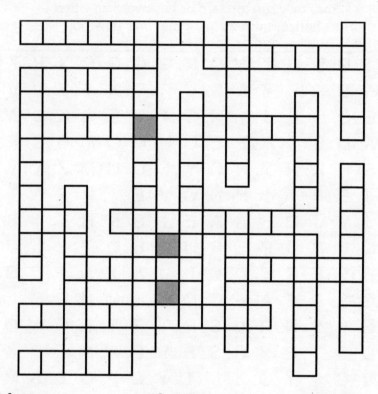

3 letters
PEA

4 letters
BEEF

5 letters
BROTH
ONION
PASTA
STOCK

6 letters
CARROT
OXTAIL
POTAGE
POTATO
TOMATO

7 letters
CHICKEN
CHOWDER
WINDSOR

8 letters
ALPHABET
BEETROOT
CONSOMME
GAZPACHO

9 letters
PEPPER POT
VEGETABLE

10 letters
MINESTRONE

11 letters
COCK-A-LEEKIE

Which four shapes (two black and two white) can be fitted together to form the dove shown here? The pieces may be rotated, but not flipped over.

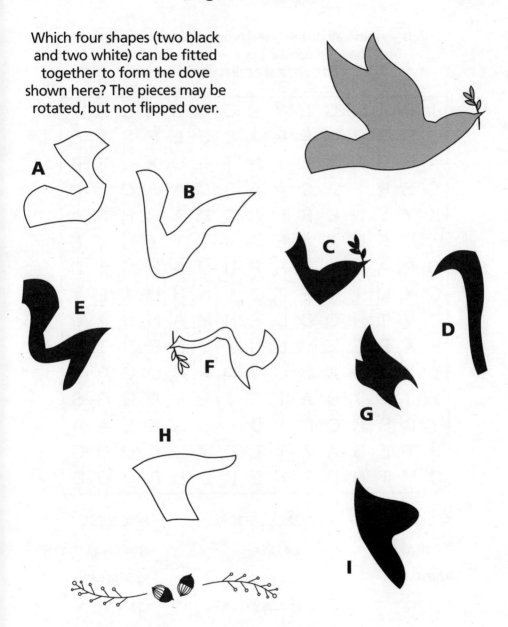

A

B

C

D

E

F

G

H

I

J

"Materialism is the only form of distraction from true bliss."

Douglas Horton

Can you find all of the listed words hidden in the grid?
They may run forward or backward, in either a
horizontal, vertical or diagonal direction.

```
I  P  E  A  C  E  Y  K  O  C  S  A  B  A  T
J  D  S  Z  M  P  R  I  C  E  L  E  S  S  S
A  S  O  W  Y  E  I  N  T  L  U  X  O  R  E
C  E  R  L  J  Q  A  A  B  M  A  S  O  I  R
K  Y  Y  N  E  B  F  S  Q  M  A  R  H  S  A
W  V  R  O  A  A  E  L  V  T  Y  Y  C  V  E
O  P  A  N  N  X  H  P  U  U  S  R  F  I  D
O  X  M  I  Y  F  T  Z  L  N  H  U  I  L  Y
D  V  T  R  O  D  D  E  N  M  A  N  R  A  U
B  A  E  E  Z  C  U  N  X  U  D  R  H  T  M
L  X  T  D  X  Q  C  V  Q  A  N  O  O  R  A
Y  J  I  I  B  A  I  C  I  L  E  F  Q  S  S
Y  C  B  R  O  D  I  D  L  O  G  L  L  A  A
H  T  E  B  A  Z  I  L  E  N  E  E  U  Q  B
O  Y  T  H  G  I  L  E  D  E  L  B  U  O  D
```

ALL GOLD	JACK WOOD	PRICELESS
ASHRAM	LATINA	QUEEN ELIZABETH
BRIDE	LEGEND	RIO SAMBA
DEAREST	LUNA ROSA	SEXY REXY
DENMAN	LUXOR	TABASCO
DOUBLE DELIGHT	MARY ROSE	THE FAIRY
FELICIA	MYRIAM	TIBET
IDOLE	PEACE	TRUST

Discover a path through the maze to reach the light!
Start at the entrance at the top of the maze.

"Life always has an unhappy ending, but you can have a lot of fun along the way, and everything doesn't have to be dripping in deep significance."

Roger Ebert

One of these barrels of apples is different from the rest. Can you spot the odd one out?

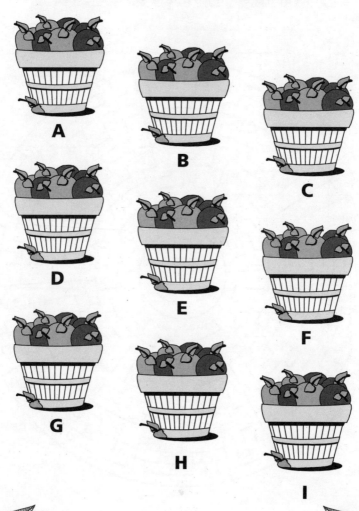

A

B

C

D

E

F

G

H

I

"As I've grown older, the simple pleasure of sitting on the couch with someone you love and watching a documentary is about as good as it gets for me."

Paul Wesley

The words are provided, but can you fit them all in the grid?

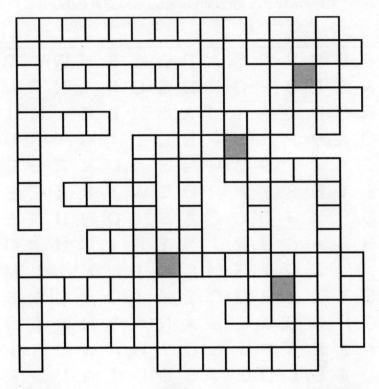

4 letters
COOL
FALL
HATS
MIST
PODS
RAIN

5 letters
ACORN
CROPS
FOGGY
FRUIT
SCARF

SEEDS
WINDY
YIELD

6 letters
APPLES
ASTERS
GLOOMY
GOLDEN

7 letters
OCTOBER
ORCHARD
ROSEHIP
STORING

9 letters
DECIDUOUS
HALLOWEEN
MUSHROOMS

10 letters
MICHAELMAS

Can you find all of the listed words hidden in the grid?
They may run forward or backward, in either a
horizontal, vertical or diagonal direction.

```
E C S C P S A P W C R H W T G
N E E B F G E B S Q P I H G N
W O R L A T U A S H B G Y A I
O A B P E S F R O L I C I R D
D A T F S B H N S N O Y R D D
E Y N S Y H R D G W Y B E E E
O E K R O C C A S I O N U N W
H F A C B E T N T P I C N I C
K V E Q I S M C C I N K I L M
E Y X S R G C E K T O R O I S
G H O O T E N A N N Y N N A O
A J E S H I N D I G W W Q S I
L J E L D Z V S O C I A L S R
A L L U A U B A N Q U E T A E
I G B I Y C E I L I D H R W E
```

BANQUET	FROLIC	REUNION
BARN DANCE	GALA	SHINDIG
BASH	GARDEN	SOCIAL
BIRTHDAY	HOEDOWN	SOIREE
CEILIDH	HOOTENANNY	SPREE
CELEBRATION	OCCASION	STAG NIGHT
FESTIVAL	PICNIC	WASSAIL
FETE	RAVE	WEDDING

Enter the answer to each clue, one letter per square, in the direction indicated by the arrows. When completed, rearrange the letters in the shaded squares to spell out a word appropriate to the theme of this book.

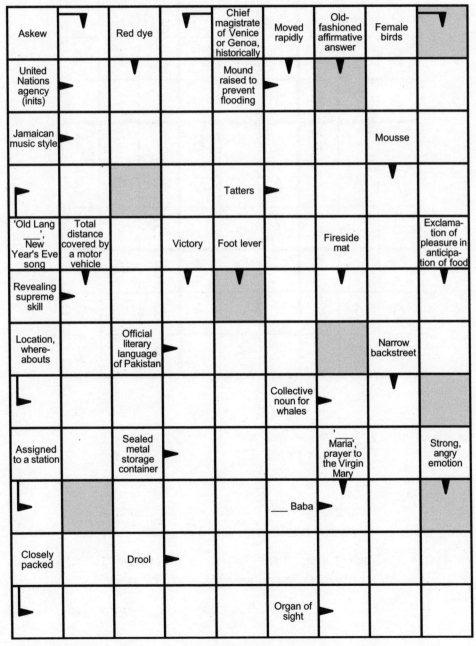

Place one of the numbers from 1 to 9 into every empty cell so that each row, each column and each 3x3 block contains all the numbers from 1 to 9.

6		3		7			2	
8		1					5	4
	7	9	1	5				
		2			8			1
7	8		4		6		9	3
3			7		5			
				4	1	6	8	
5	4					9		2
	9			6		3		7

"Nor need we power or splendor,
wide hall or lordly dome;

The good, the true, the tender
– these form wealth of home."

Sarah J. Hale

Can you find all of the listed words hidden in the grid?
They may run forward or backward, in either a
horizontal, vertical or diagonal direction.

```
S M T X Q V S L I E V E H T Y
T U O R E S C A P E Y S P Y G
O X E R I G Y Y W A E P P D Y
P Z J D L F M H V A D V E N T
G R I Y A D L O S G O R F N N
I L I D H M H E N M H K Y U E
R S B V T S A Y S T S I N Z L
L Z A F A E M Y O Y T R H E P
S R W L X T L L A E T A C L X
L G L I O V E X P E L I N O D
R I L C I M T L O C D I O G U
Q E P A A K E L I B R E L Q O
D H A C L O U D S V B S M A N
F O O R P E P K I H E L E N G
N I Q O Q R P I K Z M S I M Q
```

ADVENT	FROGS	PRIVATE LIVES
AMADEUS	GALILEO	PROOF
ATHALIE	GYPSY	SALOME
CAMELOT	HAMLET	SYLVIA
CLOUDS	HELEN	TANGO
EGMONT	LE CID	THE VEIL
ESCAPE	MEDEA	TOP GIRLS
EXILED	PLENTY	TRIFLES

The words are provided, but can you fit them all in the grid?

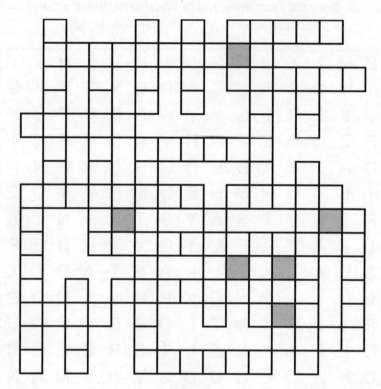

3 letters
HOP

4 letters
ARUM
HEMP
IRIS
LILY
ROSE
RUSH

5 letters
ASTER
OXLIP
POPPY
STOCK

6 letters
BRYONY
FAT HEN
NETTLE
SORREL

8 letters
ASPHODEL
DAFFODIL
PLANTAIN
PURSLANE
TOADFLAX

9 letters
DANDELION
DIAPENSIA
PIMPERNEL

10 letters
SNAPDRAGON

12 letters
LADY'S SLIPPER

Place all twelve of the pieces into the grid. Any may be rotated or flipped over, but none may touch another, not even diagonally.

The numbers outside the grid refer to the number of consecutive black squares; and each block is separated from the others by at least one white square. For instance, '3 2' could refer to a row with none, one or more white squares, then three black squares, then at least one white square, then two more black squares, followed by any number of white squares.

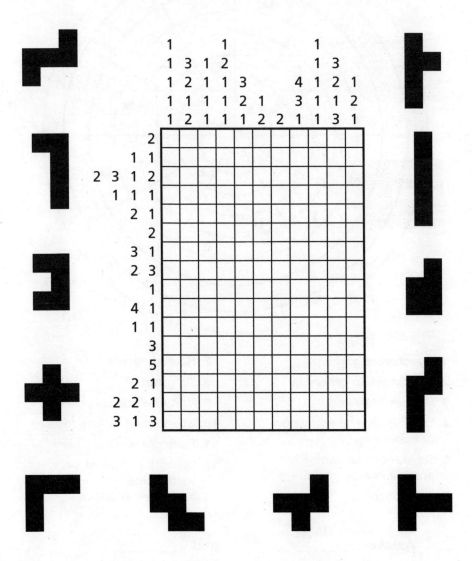

First solve the clues. All of the solutions end with the letter in the middle of the circle, and in every word an additional letter is in place. When the puzzle is complete, reading clockwise around the shaded ring of letters will reveal the names of two birds.

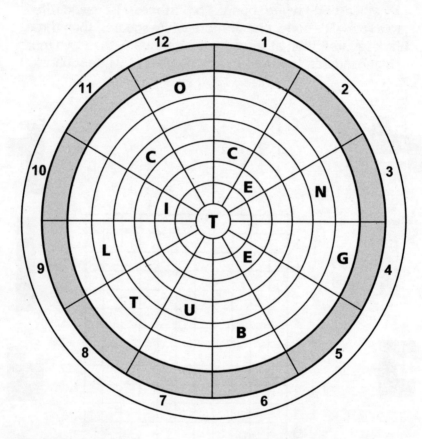

1 Waterproof garment

2 Responsive to orders

3 Financially ruined

4 Lacking general education or knowledge

5 Substance that can provide energy

6 Triumphant

7 Heated debate

8 Slingshot

9 Unit of electrical power

10 Abandoned, falling in ruins

11 Form of transport, plane

12 Cylindrical mass of earth voided by a burrowing creature

Answer: _____ **and** _____

Can you find all of the listed words hidden in the grid?
They may run forward or backward, in either a
horizontal, vertical or diagonal direction.

```
G N I N U T O K L Y S F Z T C
C B R A S S E A V G R H R E G
M W A C K F B S N X E O Z K V
A N O R P M R I Z M S H O C C
J R S O I I R F M I O T U A H
E O N T D T C S N E P H L J O
L T O E S W O C H A M B E R R
O C I N O Y I N O O O B O E U
V U T O P N R N E L C D D N S
E D C B R S V N D S O A M N A
R N E M A H B A T T E R Y I E
T O S O N J C E L L O F Y D L
U C V R O B K Z T R E C N O C
R I N T E R V A L V B W Z P B
E G R A N C A S A E P L N N J
```

BARITONE	CONDUCTOR	SCORE
BATTERY	DINNER JACKET	SECTIONS
BRASS	GRAN CASA	SOPRANO
CELLO	INTERVAL	STRINGS
CHAMBER	LEADER	TIMBAL
CHORUS	OVERTURE	TROMBONE
COMPOSER	PICCOLO	TUNING
CONCERT	ROSIN	WOODWIND

The words are provided, but can you fit them all in the grid?

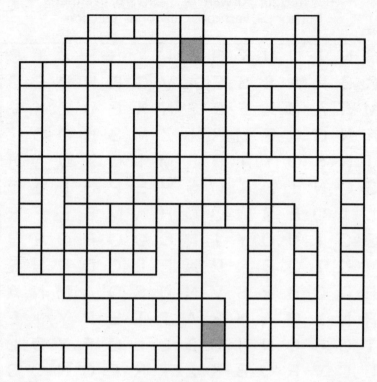

4 letters
CATS
DOGS

5 letters
CAKES
CANDY

6 letters
GRANNY
HORSES
SWEETS

7 letters
FLOWERS
INCENSE
KITTENS
SEAFOOD
WALKING

8 letters
DIAMONDS
GOOD FOOD
WEDDINGS

9 letters
CHAMPAGNE
CHRISTMAS
OPEN FIRES
SURPRISES

10 letters
TELEVISION

11 letters
SANDCASTLES

Only two of these sail boats are identical in every way. Can you spot the matching pair?

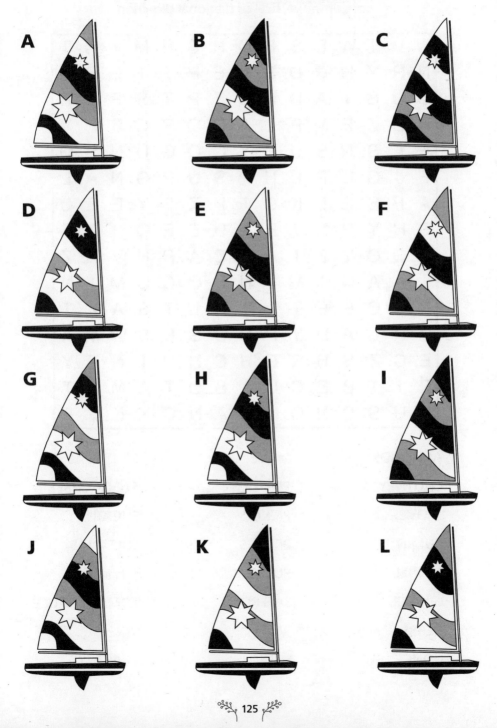

Wordsearch: PANTRY CONTENTS

Can you find all of the listed words hidden in the grid?
They may run forward or backward, in either a
horizontal, vertical or diagonal direction.

```
W V I W E B E Q H S E M Y H T
N R Y H C D S A E P T I L P S
O U S I A D R S F P T S F L E
R E Z E M P L A O O R C E P V
F A S R B U E Y G Q G U N S O
F J G U P U H P S U R G N A L
A F S E L K C I P Z S Y E E C
S H Y P N T B K U E E Q L Z S
G Q O Y Z I A M C A R H V A Z
I A A N W M V N S O C U M I N
N C C E E T L T A L T S A L T
G R L A D Y P U O S E S W M X
E C Z S B R E H C H U T N E Y
R I T B E C U A S O T A M O T
P U S D N O M L A N C X K T F
```

ALMONDS   MACE   SPLIT PEAS

CHUTNEY   PEPPER   STOCK CUBES

CLOVES   PICKLES   SUGAR

CUMIN   PRUNES   SULTANAS

FENNEL   PULSES   THYME

GINGER   SAFFRON   TOMATO SAUCE

HERBS   SALT   VINEGAR

HONEY   SOUP   YEAST

Discover a path through the maze to find your prize, a warm slice of cherry pie!

Start at the entrance at the top of the maze.

"Reflect upon your present blessings
of which every man has many –
not on your past misfortunes, of
which all men have some."

Charles Dickens

The words are provided, but can you fit them all in the grid?

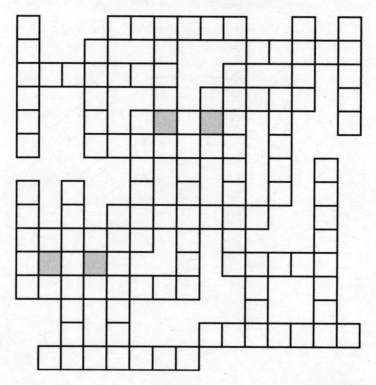

4 letters
PURL
ROWS
WOOL

5 letters
HANKS
NYLON
PLAIN
SOCKS
SPOOL
TWIST
YARNS

6 letters
CAST ON
COLLAR
JUMPER
REPEAT

7 letters
DROPPED
SELVAGE
SQUARES
SWEATER
TANK TOP
TENSION

8 letters
KNITTING
PRESSING
PULLOVER
STOCKING

9 letters
WAISTCOAT

Place all twelve of the pieces into the grid. Any may be rotated or flipped over, but none may touch another, not even diagonally.

The numbers outside the grid refer to the number of consecutive black squares; and each block is separated from the others by at least one white square. For instance, '3 2' could refer to a row with none, one or more white squares, then three black squares, then at least one white square, then two more black squares, followed by any number of white squares.

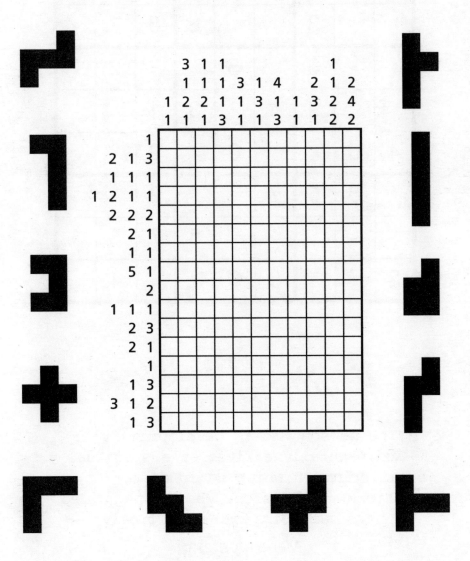

Sudoku

Place one of the numbers from 1 to 9 into every empty cell so that each row, each column and each 3x3 block contains all the numbers from 1 to 9.

	1			4	2			6
9	6	2	5					
		3			6	8	7	
		6		5			2	7
		9	4		3	1		
4	5			6		9		
	8	5	7			2		
					8	7	5	1
2			9	3			4	

"The person who is developing freely and naturally arrives at a spiritual equilibrium in which he is master of his actions, just as one who has acquired physical poise can move freely."

Maria Montessori

Can you find all of the listed words hidden in the grid?
They may run forward or backward, in either a
horizontal, vertical or diagonal direction.

```
S O S E T O N E R U T C E L H
R D G T E V E P I C E R G D C
J J R I V R N D O W A S A W B
T O Z A F E U V B I J I S C N
E O U W C T N T X L L R S A O
R R D R U Y T V A L D E E L Y
O E H O N G A A E N K C M V U
C P D P L A R D G L G E T P B
S A R N A I L E H E O I O O Q
C P E J I R S A E T M P S S R
I M P D A M G T B T R T E T E
S A O O I O E O T E I I O C N
U X R N I A J R T R L N B A N
M E T D Y L R N M U J S G R A
D D R A C U O Y K N A H T D B
```

AUTOGRAPH	GREETING	RECEIPT
BANNER	JOURNAL	RECIPE
BIRTHDAY CARD	LABELS	REMINDER
DIARY	LECTURE NOTES	REPORT
ENVELOPE	LETTER	SIGNATURE
ESSAY	MESSAGE	THANK-YOU CARD
EXAM PAPER	MUSIC SCORE	TO-DO LIST
GIFT TAG	POSTCARD	WILL

The words are provided, but can you fit them all in the grid?

4 letters
BILL
FISH
MEAL
MEAT
MENU

5 letters
GLASS
GRILL
PARTY
SEATS
SWEET

6 letters
DINERS
DINNER
DRINKS
EATERY
NAPKIN
WAITER

7 letters
CUTLERY
STARTER

8 letters
LUNCHEON
WAITRESS

9 letters
BRASSERIE

10 letters
MAIN COURSE
VEGETARIAN

Which four shapes (two black and two white) can be fitted together to form the leaf shown here? The pieces may be rotated, but not flipped over.

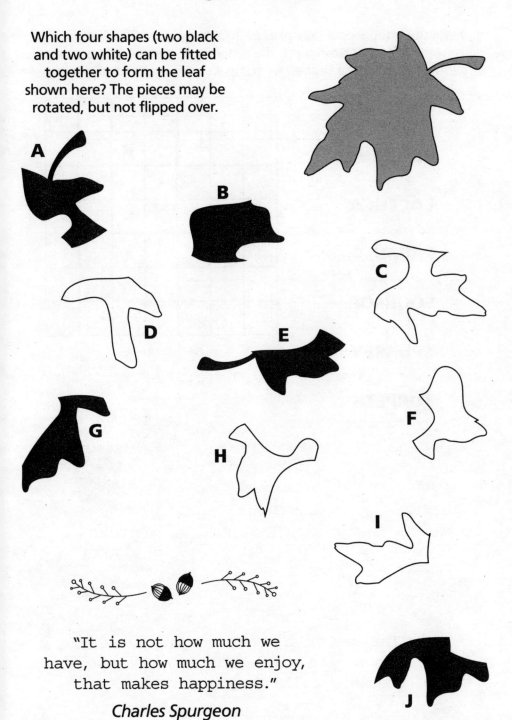

A

B

C

D

E

F

G

H

I

J

"It is not how much we have, but how much we enjoy, that makes happiness."

Charles Spurgeon

Place the listed words horizontally into the grid, so that when read from top left to bottom right, the letters in the shaded squares spell out the name of a vegetable. Some letters are already in place.

BRINJAL

HENBANE

LACTUCA

PRIMULA

SOURSOP

SPURREY

TURPETH

"The key is to keep company only with people who uplift you, whose presence calls forth your best."

Epictetus

Can you find all of the listed words hidden in the grid?
They may run forward or backward, in either a
horizontal, vertical or diagonal direction.

```
A K Y S Z N O W Y L L I D G B
L C R T E Q W Y R B O R A G E
L H E J K M F S R A L T B E G
I I L O C E A I U N O C T M D
N V E H N G R S C N B I G T N
A L C N E I L L E E E N A U C
V S E S H A M B Q S R N A N I
A L E W Q Q L U C C G A L C N
Q T M O S E C L C E A M L A C
D X Y R X A O A L Q M O S S D
A Z H T C V F I P D O N P S E
N J T Y E A C F G E T H I I R
I M U S T A R D R H R T C A F
S F M V J Z X O I O L A E Y O
E S E V I H C V L J N G H R V
```

ALLSPICE	CHIVES	NUTMEG
ANGELICA	CINNAMON	SAFFRON
ANISE	CLOVES	SAGE
BERGAMOT	CUMIN	SENNA
BORAGE	CURRY	SESAME
CAPER	DILL	ST JOHN'S WORT
CASSIA	FENNEL	THYME
CELERY	MUSTARD	VANILLA

The words are provided, but can you fit them all in the grid?

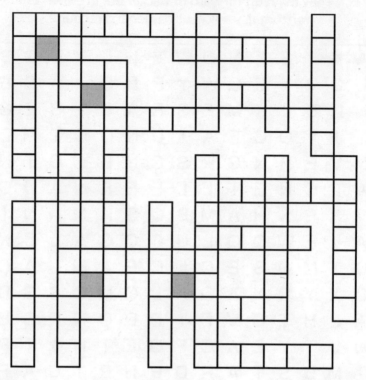

4 letters
PLUG
SINK
SOAP
SUDS

5 letters
BIDET
FLOSS
FLUSH
RAZOR

6 letters
HOT TAP
LOOFAH
MAKE-UP
MOUSSE
SPONGE

7 letters
AEROSOL
BATH MAT
BATHTUB
CABINET
CISTERN
COLOGNE

FLANNEL
SHAMPOO

9 letters
HAIRBRUSH

10 letters
TOOTHBRUSH
TOOTHPASTE

Ladle the letters from the soup tureen and fit one into each of the 26 bowls on the table below, so that the finished result is a complete crossword containing English words. All of the letters in the tureen must be used – thus no letter is used more than once. When rearranged, the letters in the filled bowls spell out a variety of apple.

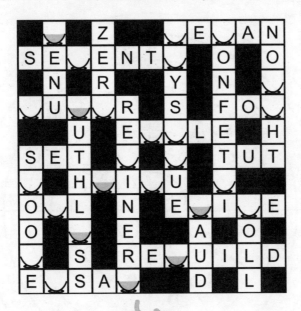

A B C D E F G H I J K
L M N O P Q R S
T U V W X Y Z

"He has achieved success who has lived well, laughed often and loved much...."

Bessie Stanley

First solve the clues. All of the solutions end with the letter in the middle of the circle, and in every word an additional letter is in place. When the puzzle is complete, reading clockwise around the shaded ring of letters will reveal the names of two birds.

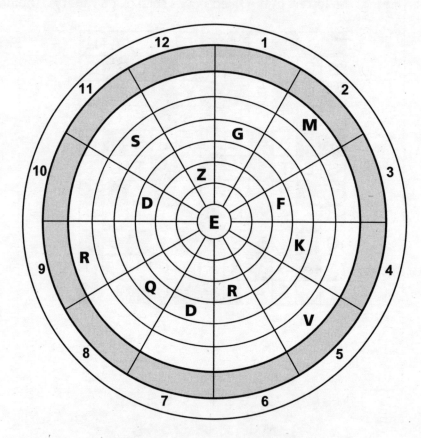

1 Means of verbal communication

2 Inoculate against disease

3 Implement for shaping, used in manicure (4,4)

4 Chain worn as an ornament

5 All people

6 Largest of the Canary Islands

7 Lower jawbone

8 Enough

9 Receive an academic degree

10 Heaven

11 Protect from heat, cold, noise, etc

12 Appropriate (especially money) fraudulently for one's own use

Answer: _____ **and** _____

Can you find all of the listed words hidden in the grid?
They may run forward or backward, in either a
horizontal, vertical or diagonal direction.

```
N I K E M A R T R G K Q G Q B
Y S E Y R E Z E E R F T R X G
Q T E F K Z C V X P R E A S L
T R L Q I I C I Q I P C T I A
E A T C U N L R H I M E E E D
A I T J N A K T E T S D R V L
S N E D R Y V D O D Q T O E E
P E K D Y Y I P A P N E O O A
O R E T G S A U C E P A N V F
O R K E H E G K T P R N L H E
N G N A T J I R T F K B P O N
N H S C K S I H W Z N L I B C
L S P U O J U F I S H F O R K
S O U P B O W L S E V L E H S
Y X C I C O F F E E C U P B H
```

BREAD KNIFE	KETTLE	SOUP BOWL
COFFEE CUP	LADLE	STOVE
COLANDER	LARDER	STRAINER
FISH FORK	PIE DISH	TEACUP
FOOD MIXER	RAMEKIN	TEAPOT
FREEZER	SAUCEPAN	TEASPOON
GRATER	SHELVES	TRIVET
JUICER	SIEVE	WHISK

132   Pyragram

Every clue in this puzzle is an anagram leading to a single-word solution. Correctly solve the anagram on each level of the pyramid and another word will appear, reading down the central column of bricks.

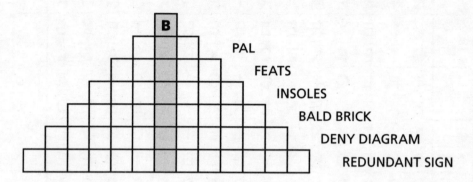

PAL

FEATS

INSOLES

BALD BRICK

DENY DIAGRAM

REDUNDANT SIGN

133   Word Wheel

Using the letters in the Wordwheel, you have ten minutes to find as many words as possible of three letters or more, none of which may be plurals, foreign words or proper nouns. Each word must contain the central letter and no letters can be used more than once per word unless they appear in different spokes of the wheel. There is at least one nine-letter word to be found.

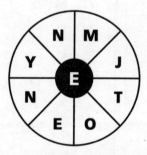

Nine-letter word(s):

_____

"True contentment is not having everything, but in being satisfied with everything you have."

Oscar Wilde

Arroword

Enter the answer to each clue, one letter per square, in the direction indicated by the arrows. When completed, rearrange the letters in the shaded squares to spell out a word appropriate to the theme of this book.

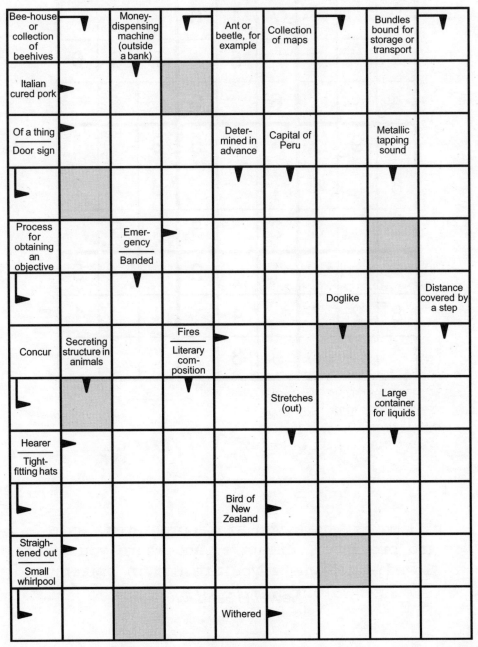

Place one of the numbers from 1 to 9 into every
empty cell so that each row, each column and each
3x3 block contains all the numbers from 1 to 9.

9			7	1	8			
1				5		7	6	9
4			6		9			
	9		4		5	8		
6		4				3		2
		8	2		3		5	
			1		2			5
8	2	7		4				1
			9	3	7			8

"Home is where you are appreciated, safe
and protected, creative, and where you are
loved – not where you are put in prison."

Nawal El Saadawi

Can you find all of the listed words hidden in the grid?
They may run forward or backward, in either a
horizontal, vertical or diagonal direction.

```
O N I K G N Y V G N B D A H M
W E H W P T O F O G N A M A Q
O D C M I B F M O N G B T Z F
X R R O X K E L M H O A F E B
N Z A B C L D E R I U Q I L E
A G E N H O A Q J Q S Z L N N
C S P O G T N Y M Y M R B U I
E N I G R E B U A A Z W E T T
P O L I V E K Q T P F A R P N
I L G X D J W J U R A Y T Z E
E E Q V I C T O R I A P L U M
N M U G O U Q A N C N D A T E
U H I A U H U I Y O J C X D L
R F L L U S D I F T L S E P C
P L G R A P E F R U I T U Z T
```

APRICOT	HAZELNUT	ORANGE
AUBERGINE	KIWI	PAPAYA
CLEMENTINE	KUMQUAT	PEAR
COCONUT	LEMON	PECAN
DATE	LIME	PERSIMMON
FIG	MANGO	PRUNE
FILBERT	MELON	QUINCE
GRAPEFRUIT	OLIVE	VICTORIA PLUM

The words are provided, but can you fit them all in the grid?

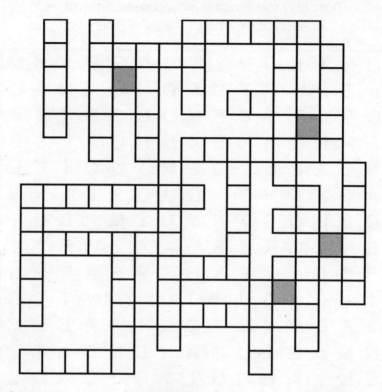

4 letters
BARS
CAKE
DARK
MILK
RICH

5 letters
CANDY
CHIPS
COCOA
FUDGE
PLAIN
SAUCE
SWEET

6 letters
BITTER
DOUBLE
ECLAIR
FONDUE
KISSES
SMOOTH

7 letters
BISCUIT
CARAMEL
LIQUEUR
TRUFFLE

8 letters
BEVERAGE
BROWNIES

9 letters
DIGESTIVE

Discover a path through the maze to find the knitting,
and relax by making a pair of mittens!

Start at the entrance at the top of the maze.

"To be content doesn't mean you
don't desire more, it means you're
thankful for what you have and
patient for what's to come."

Tony Gaskins

Patchwork Quilt

Place all twelve of the pieces into the grid. Any may be rotated or flipped over, but none may touch another, not even diagonally.

The numbers outside the grid refer to the number of consecutive black squares; and each block is separated from the others by at least one white square. For instance, '3 2' could refer to a row with none, one or more white squares, then three black squares, then at least one white square, then two more black squares, followed by any number of white squares.

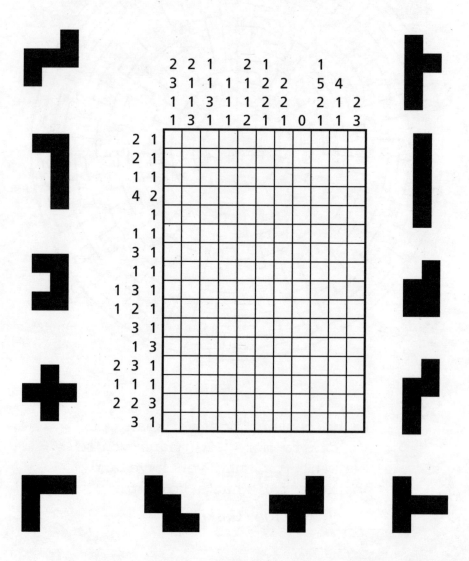

Can you find all of the listed words hidden in the grid?
They may run forward or backward, in either a
horizontal, vertical or diagonal direction.

```
V P E G E U G A E L L O C V T
I R N C B X L I R E A O E S E
E T A M I T N I E H E T I D S
A E T F E L E A E U A L A B H
I N J R A O P L P M A R C R P
D P E B O M J M M Y M X O O S
N G A D F H I O O O U S M T U
O F N R E V O L C C I J P H P
I M B Z T R Y C I S C X A E P
N M D F R N R N T A A A T R O
A B U F E A E E O O R D R G R
P U A H Y L R R S R W Z I I T
M D V I C L L K U O C M O E E
O D S Q L Y S O H Y A V T G R
C Y B T W E L L W I S H E R L
```

ACCOMPLICE	COLLEAGUE	INTIMATE
ALLY	COMPANION	LOVER
ALTER EGO	COMPATRIOT	LOYALIST
AMIGO	COMPEER	PARTNER
BROTHER	COMRADE	ROOMMATE
BUDDY	CRONY	SISTER
CHUM	FAMILIAR	SUPPORTER
COHORT	FELLOW	WELL-WISHER

The words are provided, but can you fit them all in the grid?

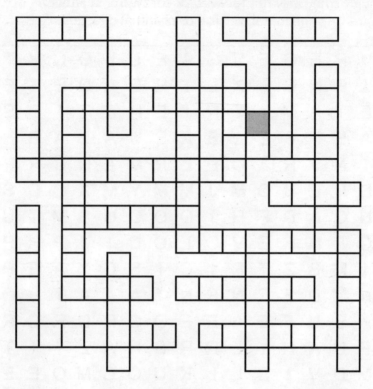

4 letters
MACE
SAGE
SALT
SOUP

5 letters
CUMIN
HONEY
SUGAR
YEAST

6 letters
FENNEL
GINGER
NUTMEG
PEPPER
PICKLE
PRUNES

7 letters
MUSTARD
RAISINS
TREACLE

8 letters
STUFFING
TARRAGON

9 letters
SPLIT PEAS

10 letters
DRIED FRUIT
SALAD CREAM
STOCK CUBES

Codeword 142

Every letter in this crossword has been replaced by a number, the number remaining the same for that letter wherever it occurs. Can you substitute numbers for letters and complete the crossword?

Some letters have already been entered into the grid, to help you on your way. When finished, use the code to spell out the name of a butterfly.

A	14	9	25	13	20	■	5	20	21	11	22	9	6	N
B	16	■	2	■	13	■	13	■	15	■	20	■	20	O
C	11	1	10	13	17	25	26	■	2	2	13	12	13	P
D	20	■	3	■	21	■	26	■	3	■	1	■	11	Q
E	19	25	1	6	20	3	2	21	24	11	3	14	12	R
F	18	■	■	13	■	■	25	■	11	■	6	■	13	S
G	■	8	3	23	25	2	■	4	25	5	25	2	■	T
H	12	■	12	■	16	■	10	■	■	25	■	■	7	U
I	13	8	8	20	21	8	20	3	13	6	3	21	1	V
J	20	■	25	■	1	■	3	■	16	■	22	■	3	W
K	6	21	20	14	21	■	25	13	20	8	2	11	22	X
L	18	■	3	■	12	■	1	■	25	■	21	■	9	Y
M	20	25	2	13	18	25	26	■	14	9	21 O	20 R	6 T	Z

1	2	3	4	5	6 T	7	8	9	10	11	12	13
14	15	16	17	18	19	20 R	21 O	22	23	24	25	26

Answer

8	25	13	16	21	16	7

One of these candles is different from the rest. Can you spot the odd one out?

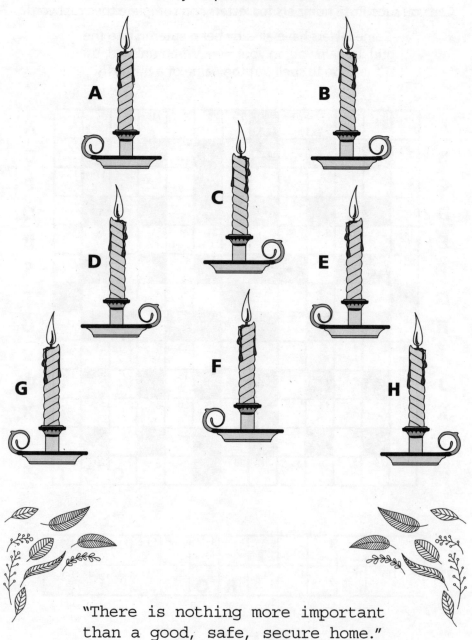

"There is nothing more important than a good, safe, secure home."

Rosalynn Carter

Can you find all of the lines from the poem *Little Things* by Ebenezer Cobham Brewer hidden in the grid? They may run forward or backward, in either a horizontal, vertical or diagonal direction.

```
L F O I X E H T E K A M Y S M
H I T L H L H U V E O O M N Y
S U T H I F E N M E Z V S A T
P O P T E T E T I B E I E S I
O I U E L Y T G H H L Y G A N
R H H B Y E B L T U O E A E R
D G G J R S M E E C S V Y L E
E J K U T U K I T G W T T P T
L R B C O A G N N H R C H Z E
T E E E M H A X G U Y A G E F
T E I T E S T A N A T M I I O
I O U C A H E F Z O H E M N E
L K F E A W R H C H G X S H S
R A L S M V F E I F I H T W G
I P N P A E A O P G M D P E A
N Y Q D K N A U I V N J G U S
A S E F I G D W F A Y I F I F
```

Little drops	Ocean	Humble
Of water,	And the	Though
Little grains	Pleasant	They be,
Of sand,	Land.	Make the
Make the	Thus the	Mighty ages
Mighty	Little minutes,	Of eternity.

The words are provided, but can you fit them all in the grid?

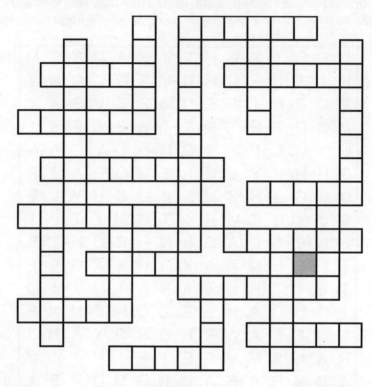

4 letters
CAFE
LAKE

5 letters
FENCE
GRASS
LAWNS
PATHS
PONDS
ROSES
SEATS
SWANS
TREES

6 letters
AVIARY
BUSHES
PEOPLE
SEESAW
STATUE
TENNIS

7 letters
BENCHES
FLOWERS

8 letters
FOUNTAIN
PAVILION

9 letters
BANDSTAND

10 letters
PLAYGROUND

Columns

Place the answers in order across the horizontal rows.
When completed correctly, reading down each of the
shaded columns will reveal the name of a plant.

1 Blossomed
2 Sugar found in fruit and honey
3 Throw overboard
4 Advancement
5 Aromatic bark of a tree
   used as a spice
6 Alert, watchful
7 Bushy-tailed arboreal rodent
8 Purple gemstone

"We must let go of the
life we have planned,
so as to accept the one
that is waiting for us."

Joseph Campbell

Flower Power

Fit the listed words into the grid below (one letter is already in place), then rearrange the letters in the shaded squares to form the name of a flower.

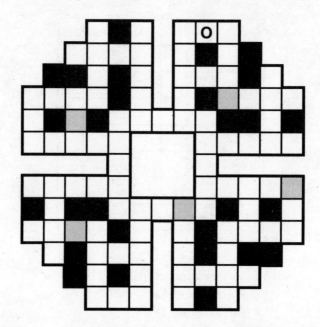

3 letters	4 letters		5 letters	
APE	BARB	OOZE	BANJO	ROWED
DID	BEAN	PITY	BEIGE	SALTY
DOT	BRAE	SOYA	CLAMP	TWIST
NOT	DOSE	TERM	DOGMA	VALET
PEN	EVER	USED	ERECT	VOICE
POP	MENU	YARD	PANIC	WHEAT
SAG				
SHE				

"Just living is not enough... one must have sunshine, freedom, and a little flower."

Hans Christian Andersen

Can you find all of the listed words hidden in the grid?
They may run forward or backward, in either a
horizontal, vertical or diagonal direction.

```
E R S S E N S S E L E M I T E
Z E E E V I T C E P S R E P S
S V I G I L A N C E S E M F C
A H T I A C W V H K E R F O T
N L F H T R Q I I K N A N N H
C P U U G L D S S F C C E D O
T U F F Y I W I Z D E M M R U
U G O U D T L O X N O Q O S G
A N C F R E I N T M S M G B H
R I U R B W E R E F N N G S T
Y N S E Y X A H A R I M P L F
O E O E F T T Y M L H A Q P U
Z P U D I N D L E F C A Q O L
T O L O I H A E P E A C E M G
H K N M V C F Y T I N E R E S
```

CALM	HEEDFUL	SERENITY
CARE	IN THE MOMENT	SOUL
CLARITY	LIGHT	SPACE
CONCENTRATION	OPENING UP	THOUGHTFUL
ESSENCE	PEACE	TIMELESSNESS
FEELINGS	PERSPECTIVE	VIGILANCE
FOCUS	REGARD	VISION
FREEDOM	SANCTUARY	WISDOM

Do It Yourself

Straightforward clues are presented with the crossword grid but the clues are in alphabetical order and the grid is minus its black squares. You need to black out some of the squares, resulting in a filled symmetrical crossword, as well as fill in the missing letters. When finished, rearrange the letters in the shaded squares (which must not be blacked out) to spell out the name of a wild flower.

I	C	E	B	E	R	▓	E	M	O	T	T	O
C	H	E	E	R	E	D	C	O	V	E	R	S
D	I	E	T	A	M	U	R	D	E	R	▓	R
S	N	O	W	Y	A	M	U	E	R	A	M	P
C	A	R	E	▓	R	E	E	R	T	U	B	E
O	B	R	E	A	K	I	L	N	O	S	L	Y
A	G	▓	N	Y	I	N	K	W	A	▓	E	R
T	R	A	I	N	T	Y	P	I	C	A	L	O
S	A	G	A	O	E	▓	E	R	C	I	S	E
S	N	O	R	T	N	A	S	O	O	T	H	S
T	I	R	E	S	O	M	E	N	U	P	▓	N
S	T	U	N	A	N	I	T	A	N	G	V	E
P	E	D	A	▓	I	P	A	N	T	H	E	R

Acute pain

Amid

Coarse-grained rock, often pink

Criminal who commits homicide

Favourite saying of a sect or political group

Former Spanish monetary unit

High-quality porcelain

Hollow cylinder

Lacking mercy

Large feline of tropical America

Large mass of frozen water

Lever operated with the foot

Long detailed story

Keep fit, work out

Make mention of

Open and observable

Prescribed selection of foods

Projection shaped to fit into a mortise

Push roughly

Shake with fear

Situated at the top of

Statement

Structure for open-air sports

Tedious

Unworried

Vacillate

> "Happiness is very simple and minimal."
>
> *Tablo*

First solve the clues. All of the solutions end with the letter in the middle of the circle, and in every word an additional letter is in place. When the puzzle is complete, reading clockwise around the shaded ring of letters will reveal a word appropriate to the theme of this book.

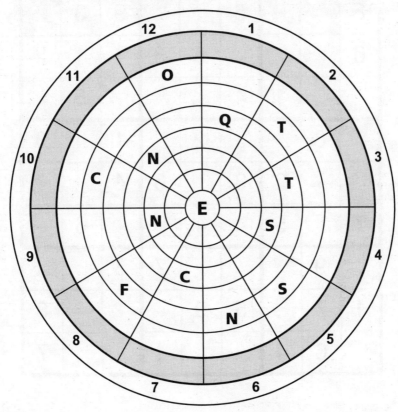

1 Sufficient
2 Free from a twisted state
3 Slow-moving reptile
4 Good-looking
5 Rough guess
6 Having no intelligible meaning
7 Be prudent or watchful (4,4)

8 Having no limits in time, space or magnitude
9 Start
10 Addition
11 Three-sided figure
12 National Park in California, famed for its waterfalls

Answer: _____

Place one of the numbers from 1 to 9 into every
empty cell so that each row, each column and each
3x3 block contains all the numbers from 1 to 9.

8			6			9	3	
6				5	3		1	2
		1	4				5	
	8			2		1		3
		2	3		6	4		
7		5		4			6	
	9				7	3		
1	7		5	9				8
	6	4			1			7

"A determined pursuit of happiness doesn't
necessarily lead to well-being. At the heart
of Danish life, and at the core of hygge,
is the deeper stability of contentment."

Louisa Thomsen Brits

Can you find all of the lines from the poem *Song from Pippa Passes* by Robert Browning hidden in the grid? They may run forward or backward, in either a horizontal, vertical or diagonal direction.

```
E  N  N  R  O  H  T  E  H  T  N  O  Y  N  V
D  E  W  P  E  A  R  L  D  E  Y  S  O  E  N
U  K  E  B  G  C  X  X  V  R  E  I  N  K  W
K  A  X  G  T  Y  T  A  A  D  P  F  J  I  B
G  T  O  Z  A  H  E  H  I  X  E  V  T  A  T
N  S  G  Z  Q  H  G  S  E  B  V  H  T  V  H
I  E  D  H  S  G  L  I  A  S  T  M  U  E  E
R  V  S  I  Q  L  D  T  R  H  N  O  I  G  Y
P  E  H  N  I  X  T  W  E  S  M  A  N  Q  E
S  N  V  H  P  H  G  W  Y  I  L  I  I  V  A
E  G  E  A  E  G  O  A  Y  Q  W  L  E  L  R
H  H  N  M  W  R  D  W  N  E  J  P  A  M  S
T  R  O  I  L  D  S  O  H  C  C  D  K  G  A
F  R  R  D  N  A  I  T  D  L  Z  F  F  H  T
N  R  H  A  H  R  N  T  H  E  L  A  R  K  S
O  M  P  K  Z  O  O  D  T  N  N  O  I  O  T
Q  B  W  J  I  P  H  M  O  G  K  Q  Y  M  Y
```

The year's at	The lark's
The spring,	On the wing;
And day's	The snail's
At the morn;	On the thorn;
Morning's	God's in
At seven;	His heaven—
The hill-side's	All's right
Dew-pearl'd;	With the world.

Which four shapes (two black and two white) can be fitted together to form the swan shown here? The pieces may be rotated, but not flipped over.

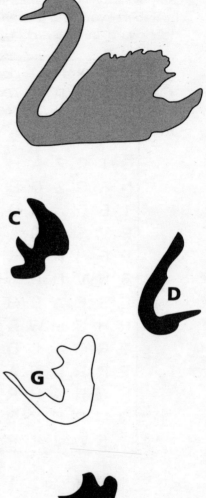

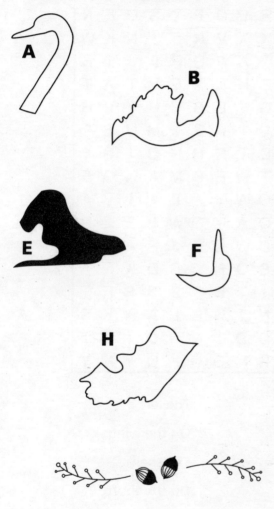

A

B

C

D

E

F

G

H

I

J

"There is just something about starting your day with something luxurious like a bath."

Erin Heatherton

The words are provided, but can you fit them all in the grid?

4 letters
BOWL
DISH
FORK
SALT

5 letters
BREAD
FRUIT
GLASS
KNIFE
LADLE
PLATE
SAUCE
SPOON

6 letters
NAPKIN
PEPPER
TUREEN

7 letters
FLOWERS
KETCHUP
MUSTARD

8 letters
PLACE MAT
WATER JUG

9 letters
LAZY SUSAN

10 letters
WINE BOTTLE

Discover a path through the maze to find your prize,
a delicious mug of cocoa overflowing with hygge!

Start at the entrance at the top of the maze.

"If you only have one smile in you,
give it to the people you love.
Don't be surly at home, then go out
in the street and start grinning
'Good morning' at total strangers."

Maya Angelou

Wordsearch: BALLETS   156

Can you find all of the listed words hidden in the grid?
They may run forward or backward, in either a
horizontal, vertical or diagonal direction.

```
N M B S A S E M A C A G O N E
J S U I T T C D B O L E R O T
X U E J U Z O P A R X C Y N O
D E N A Y A G Y R C D K U A X
F H L G N M P V B H A T P N I
I P R E A B A O D O C F O A U
R R O B C N U T L R X N E T Q
E O D T U O H C A L A E L N N
B K E A N R R C Y M O N L E O
I O O K K R K S W X F I E V D
R Z J B G E P M A L W D S A P
D N E M R A C F W I R N I L W
Z A I V L Y S E Y Y R O G O C
P T D S E C O N S E L E H S L
P E T R O U C H K A V V Q D O
```

AGON	FIREBIRD	MANON
ANYUTA	GAYANE	NUTCRACKER
APOLLO	GISELLE	ONDINE
BOLERO	JEUX	ORPHEUS
CARMEN	JOB	PETROUCHKA
CHOUT	LA VENTANA	RODEO
DON QUIXOTE	LE CORSAIRE	SYLVIA
FACADE	LES NOCES	TOY BOX

Patchwork Quilt

Place all twelve of the pieces into the grid. Any may be rotated or flipped over, but none may touch another, not even diagonally.

The numbers outside the grid refer to the number of consecutive black squares; and each block is separated from the others by at least one white square. For instance, '3 2' could refer to a row with none, one or more white squares, then three black squares, then at least one white square, then two more black squares, followed by any number of white squares.

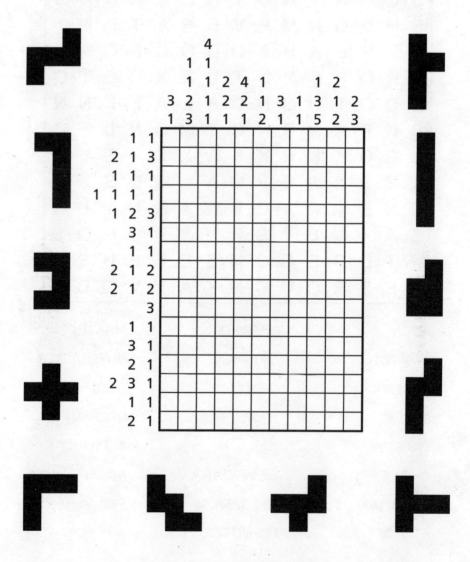

Only two of these swirling balloons are identical in every way. Can you spot the matching pair?

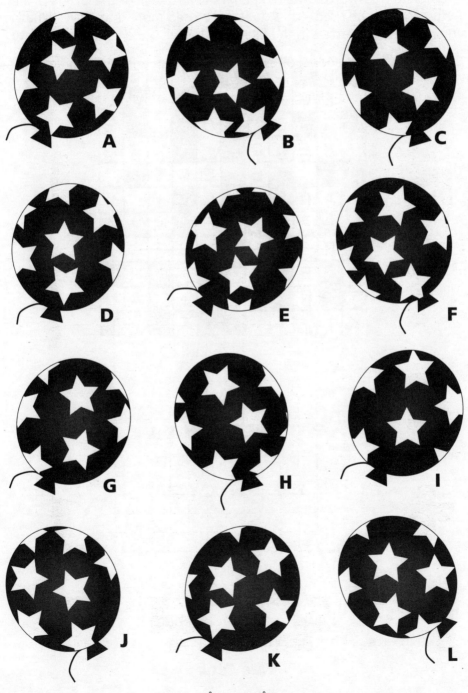

Ladle the letters from the soup tureen and fit one into each of the 26 bowls on the table below, so that the finished result is a complete crossword containing English words. All of the letters in the tureen must be used – thus no letter is used more than once. When rearranged, the letters in the filled bowls spell out a variety of tomato.

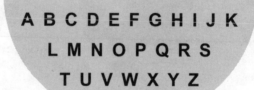

A B C D E F G H I J K

L M N O P Q R S

T U V W X Y Z

"There's a magical tie to the land
of our home, which the heart cannot
break, though the footsteps may roam."

Eliza Cook

Pyragram

Every clue in this puzzle is an anagram leading to a single-word solution. Correctly solve the anagram on each level of the pyramid and another word will appear, reading down the central column of bricks.

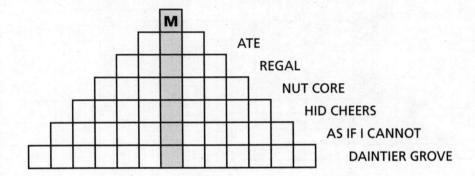

ATE

REGAL

NUT CORE

HID CHEERS

AS IF I CANNOT

DAINTIER GROVE

Word Wheel

Using the letters in the Wordwheel, you have ten minutes to find as many words as possible of three letters or more, none of which may be plurals, foreign words or proper nouns. Each word must contain the central letter and no letters can be used more than once per word unless they appear in different spokes of the wheel. There is at least one nine-letter word to be found.

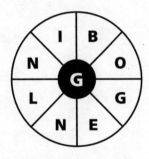

Nine-letter word(s):

_____

"The whole world is a series of miracles, but we're so used to them we call them ordinary things."

Hans Christian Andersen

SOLUTIONS

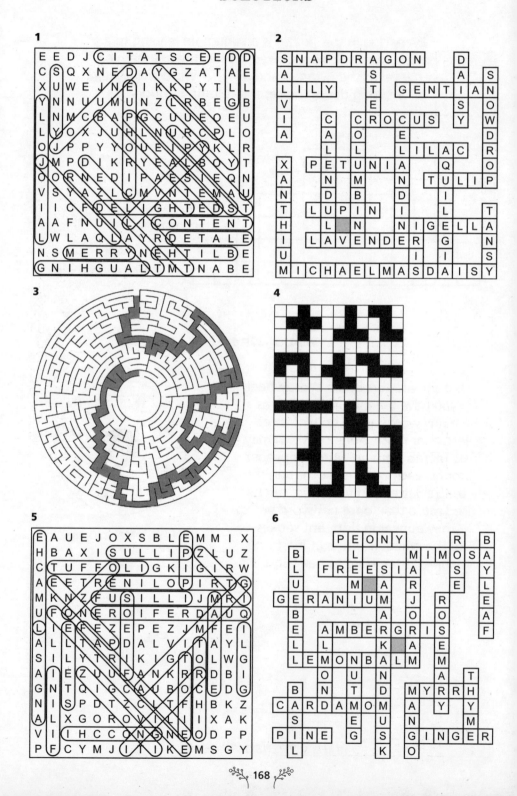

SOLUTIONS

7

1	8	6	3	2	4	5	7	9
5	3	7	9	1	8	2	4	6
2	4	9	7	5	6	3	1	8
7	2	3	5	8	9	4	6	1
6	9	5	4	3	1	7	8	2
4	1	8	2	6	7	9	3	5
3	7	1	6	9	5	8	2	4
9	6	4	8	7	2	1	5	3
8	5	2	1	4	3	6	9	7

8

1 Tolerant, 2 Ornament, 3 Greatest, 4 Eyesight, 5 Thinnest, 6 Hazelnut, 7 Explicit, 8 Resident, 9 Novelist, 10 Elephant, 11 Schubert, 12 Shortcut.
Answer: TOGETHERNESS

9

Y	T	N	E	V	E	S	W	W	W	W	F	E	O	N
B	G	A	B	T	O	M	L	O	Y	Y	D	W	I	Z
D	W	L	G	R	S	T	O	B	N	I	Y	S	E	H
E	H	O	O	E	B	E	O	R	R	S	G	F	G	A
R	I	G	Y	O	D	V	I	D	F	N	H	U	I	W
O	T	L	K	M	K	I	N	L	I	E	O	T	O	D
C	E	L	J	P	O	A	T	H	E	B	K	O	I	W
S	F	I	G	P	L	O	T	R	E	V	D	A	I	W
E	O	W	P	D	K	A	R	H	E	L	O	T	T	U
E	R	I	O	T	A	A	T	E	A	T	H	L	U	G
R	F	O	Q	N	G	Z	Q	N	L	B	S	Z	P	S
H	W	Y	D	H	D	K	D	J	L	T	Y	A	M	T
T	B	T	X	S	A	S	C	O	R	E	T	C	E	A
S	E	R	E	N	A	Y	O	H	J	S	N	I	N	N
N	F	I	F	T	Y	M	O	R	E	X	E	O	L	D
W	O	N	Y	R	R	E	H	C	U	P	W	H	L	S
L	E	P	S	G	N	I	R	P	S	Y	T	F	I	F

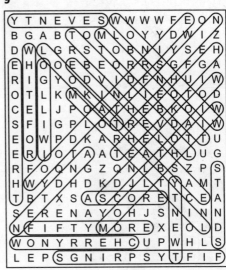

10

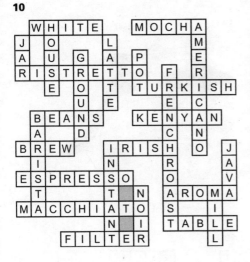

11

D: The chocolate stick is shorter.

12

C
DOE
REMIT
CONFIDE
DIPLOMACY
CELEBRATION
CONFECTIONERY

13

Nine-letters: COMMUNITY

SOLUTIONS

14

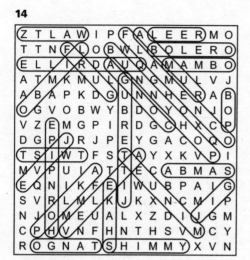

15

	Q		A		F		S	
B	U	L	L	F	I	G	H	T
	A		O	E	R		A	
B	R	U	N	T		S	P	A
	T		G	A	R	T	E	R
B	O	W			O	A	S	T
	A	S	S	A	Y		Y	
B	A	L	L	A	D		C	
	T	E	D		S	A	W	
D	O	Z	E	D		E	R	A
	I		V	E	N	E	E	R
A	L	I	E	N		P	R	Y

Answer: LOVE

16

Answer: ONWARD

17

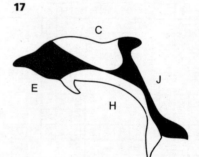

18

19

SOLUTIONS

20

6	2	8	7	9	3	1	5	4
4	5	9	2	6	1	8	7	3
1	7	3	5	4	8	6	9	2
7	6	2	3	5	9	4	1	8
5	3	4	1	8	7	2	6	9
8	9	1	4	2	6	5	3	7
3	1	5	8	7	4	9	2	6
2	8	6	9	3	5	7	4	1
9	4	7	6	1	2	3	8	5

21

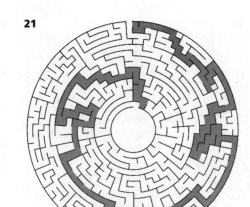

22

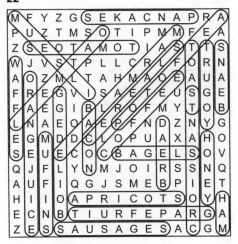

23

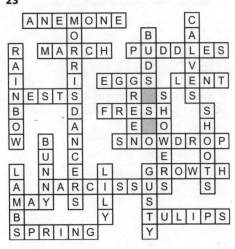

24

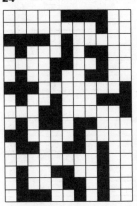

25

Answer: SWALLOWTAIL

171

SOLUTIONS

26

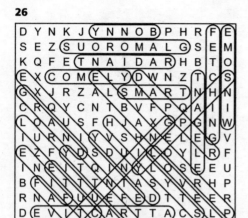

27

28

1 Pakistan, 2 Imprison, 3 Grandson,
4 Eviction, 5 Occasion, 6 Nitrogen,
7 Gershwin, 8 Optician, 9 Donation,
10 Watchman, 11 Illusion, 12 Tungsten.
Answer: PIGEON and GODWIT

29

C	L	A	V	I	C	L	E
T	O	L	E	R	A	T	E
T	A	L	I	S	M	A	N
M	U	S	H	R	O	O	M
D	I	P	L	O	M	A	T
S	H	I	L	L	I	N	G
N	I	C	H	O	L	A	S
N	E	E	D	L	E	S	S

30

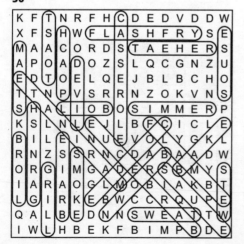

31

SOLUTIONS

32

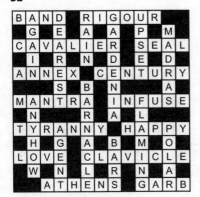

Answer: SAXIFRAGE

33

Answer: CALENDULA

34

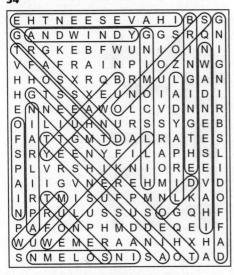

35

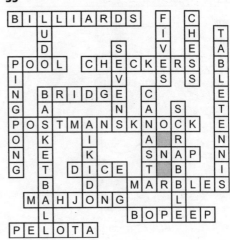

36

7	3	1	4	2	6	5	9	8
9	4	8	5	1	3	7	2	6
5	2	6	9	8	7	1	4	3
1	7	3	8	6	9	2	5	4
2	6	4	3	5	1	9	8	7
8	5	9	2	7	4	3	6	1
4	1	5	6	3	2	8	7	9
3	9	2	7	4	8	6	1	5
6	8	7	1	9	5	4	3	2

37

C	A	T	M	I	N	T
S	A	F	F	R	O	N
F	L	Y	T	R	A	P
N	I	G	E	L	L	A
A	L	K	A	N	E	T
B	U	G	B	A	N	E
L	U	C	E	R	N	E

SOLUTIONS

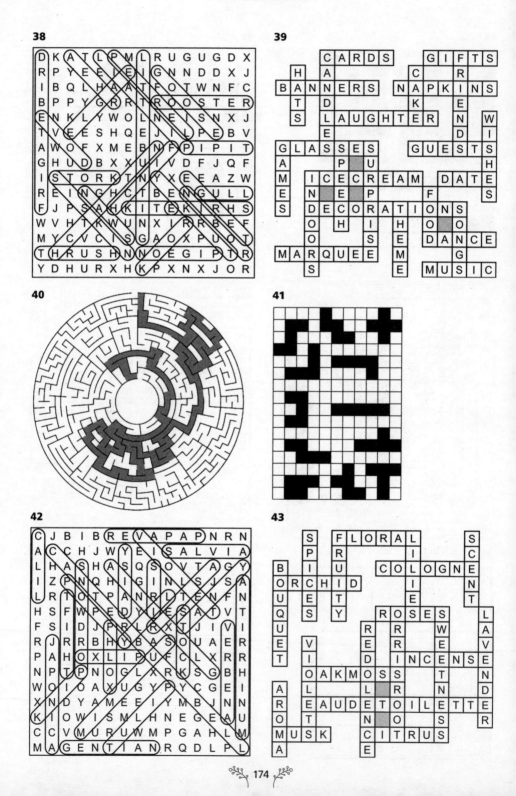

38

39

40

41

42

43

SOLUTIONS

44

A: There is one more piece of fruit.

46

1 Salesman, 2 Pantheon, 3 Ambition,
4 Reaction, 5 Romanian, 6 Oblivion,
7 Wastebin, 8 Religion, 9 Assassin,
10 Vacation, 11 Einstein, 12 Napoleon.
Answer: SPARROW and RAVEN

45

```
Y Q I B K D P T E N E S S A M
S H L D S C H E R U B I N I K
S P L Z C S H O A A C G X O C
U U E M W P U A T E Z I B L U
B R I T T E N A N S C O K L L
E C H R U D O R R D L L M A G
D E C W N E V O H T E E B V M
G L N W G Y R I L N S L D A X
O L O F F E N B A C H E S C R
U Q P V N I Z S P U C C I N I
N I D G D J S M E T A N A O V
O C A O M H X E T G M X G E Z
D W R J I T T O N E M S R L H
R O N A D R O I G M M D L Q W
B E R L I O Z S X Q I U E L Z
```

47

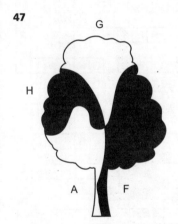

G
H
A   F

48

3	9	5	6	8	7	4	1	2
8	6	1	2	4	5	9	3	7
4	7	2	9	3	1	5	8	6
1	3	9	4	5	6	2	7	8
6	5	7	8	2	3	1	9	4
2	4	8	7	1	9	3	6	5
5	1	6	3	7	4	8	2	9
9	8	3	5	6	2	7	4	1
7	2	4	1	9	8	6	5	3

49

```
S S D L L F C H T D K W C T G
T Z P W J C E D G R A E G D R
N D R O T I U R F T A R N M T
A C T B N T K B E N M Y I R E
R L F E Y G R R U A E X L A M
R H U A Q E E D E T E A L G P
U B U T C N S R B R T S I U E
C P P I A H C A Q P N E F S R
V K P N S P W X N I T E R W A
P E S G X P S B S A R D N W T
U S N P S I O I R U T E T B U
O V E N C R A O R U O L F H R
U X U I R R C O N E M I U P E
K I N G R E D I E N T S N S M
S G G E D V Z Q K Y J F X F X
```

50

```
H     R O O F R A C K
A         L     O     P       G
T     B   Y   G U I D E       R
C A N T E E N     N     G S   O
H       A     E   T           U
E       C U T L E R Y   W O O D
T O R C H   A   Y     Y       S
        N   C                 H
R A I N   O U T D O O R S     E
  X       P   E   D     T     E
K E T T L E   R   E S C A P E
  E       N   N     T   K     T
  E       A       P O L E S
S I T E   I           V S
      G R I D D L E
```

SOLUTIONS

51
D and H

53
Nine-letters: WELLBEING

52

54
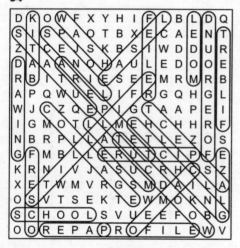

55
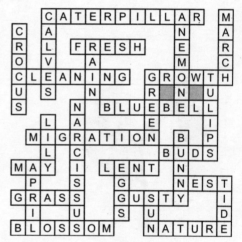

56
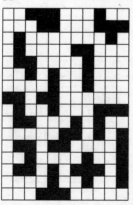

57
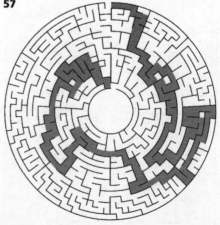

SOLUTIONS

58

59

60

Answer: FAMILY

61

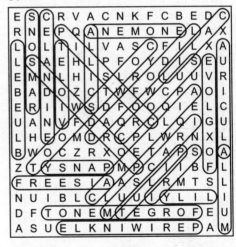

62

3	4	5	8	6	2	9	1	7
6	8	7	5	1	9	3	4	2
9	1	2	7	3	4	8	6	5
7	6	8	1	4	3	5	2	9
5	3	9	6	2	7	4	8	1
4	2	1	9	8	5	7	3	6
2	5	4	3	7	6	1	9	8
8	9	6	4	5	1	2	7	3
1	7	3	2	9	8	6	5	4

63

1 Brighter, 2 Engineer, 3 Armchair,
4 Calendar, 5 Hotelier, 6 Corridor, 7 Overhear,
8 Mediator, 9 Bachelor, 10 Interior,
11 November, 12 Gossamer.
Answer: BEACHCOMBING

SOLUTIONS

64

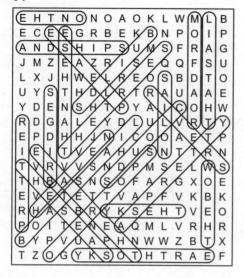

65

66

67

68

SOLUTIONS

69

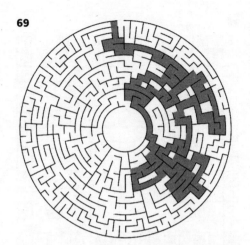

70

71

```
E T I D O R H P A T R A G U S
O T H Q C T A Y G T E Q I H A
H W B E A U T I F U L N L C F
A Y D X M K R N E O W T D R X
J E H S I R H I V U N B I E D
I N H S U L T E E E R E E A R
J T S W U U R O M I N T R F E
D I P U C R W H F D E H U A I
E E X H T D C I S O K A S R I
A T M S O A Q H T L X N A I S
N D N O T K I T T E N D E E E
G D R T P K N T N O S R S E D
E K A K W I D O G T V O T T U
L H E Y B P O M E X S M Q H U
I L Y L O V I N G A A E L Z Q
```

72

7	4	2	9	6	8	5	1	3
6	3	5	1	2	7	4	8	9
1	9	8	4	3	5	2	7	6
5	6	4	8	9	3	1	2	7
8	2	9	7	1	6	3	4	5
3	7	1	5	4	2	6	9	8
2	8	7	3	5	4	9	6	1
9	5	6	2	7	1	8	3	4
4	1	3	6	8	9	7	5	2

73

G: One of her plaits is shorter.

74

Answer: REDWING

SOLUTIONS

75

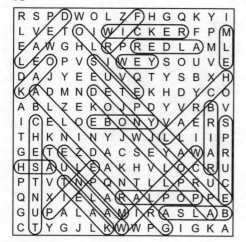

76

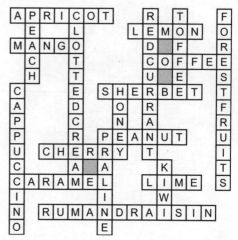

77

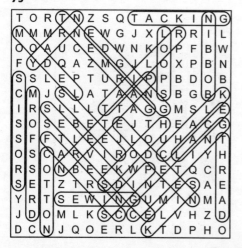

78

1 Ancestry, 2 Pharmacy, 3 Priority,
4 Recovery, 5 Equality, 6 Currency, 7 Identify,
8 Amicably, 9 Tendency, 10 Intimacy,
11 Ordinary, 12 Nativity.
Answer: APPRECIATION

79

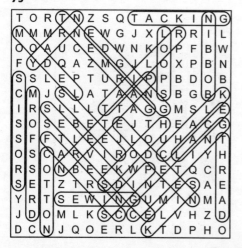

80

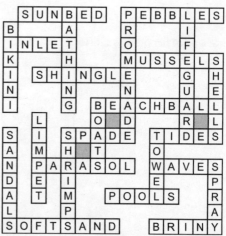

SOLUTIONS

81

Answer: NICOTIANA

82

B	A	S	I	C		M	A	C	A	Q	U	E
E		H		H		I		A		U		N
E	M	E	R	A	L	D		S	T	I	N	G
C		R		P		W		H		R		R
H	A	I	L		B	A	D		O	K	R	A
		F		J	O	Y		R				V
I	N	F	L	U	X		Z	O	M	B	I	E
N				G		P	I	T		R		
S	E	A	M		C	A	P		G	A	L	E
P		M		F		R		F		V		V
E	R	A	S	E		S	A	U	S	A	G	E
C		Z		E		O		S		D		N
T	R	E	A	S	O	N		S	C	O	U	T

Answer: CABBAGE WHITE

83

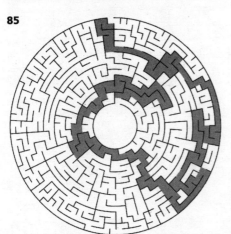

84

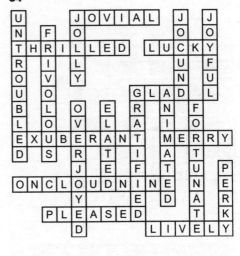

85

86

5	1	8	3	9	2	4	7	6
4	6	2	7	5	1	3	9	8
7	9	3	8	6	4	1	2	5
6	4	5	2	7	3	8	1	9
2	7	1	6	8	9	5	4	3
8	3	9	1	4	5	7	6	2
1	8	6	5	2	7	9	3	4
3	2	4	9	1	8	6	5	7
9	5	7	4	3	6	2	8	1

SOLUTIONS

87

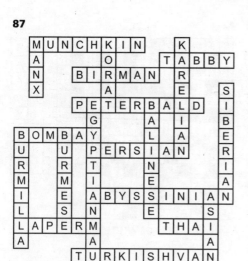

88

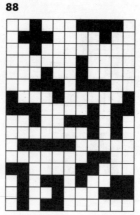

89

Answer: LARKSPUR

90

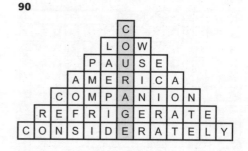

91

Nine-letters: ABUNDANCE

92

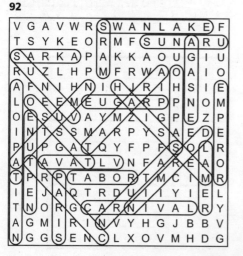

93

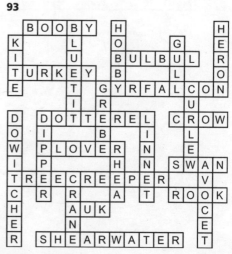

SOLUTIONS

94

	P		C		S		D	
	S	O	R	C	E	R	E	R
D	I	R	E		R		L	
	N	E	M	E	S	I	S	
	T	A	L	E	N	T		I
		T		T	E	R	S	E
A	R	E	A			A	U	G
	E		D		G	Y	B	E
B	A	L	L	S			Z	
	S	U	I		P	R	E	Y
	O	R	B		A	U	R	A
O	N	E		E	L	B	O	W

Answer: INTIMACY

95

1 Fabulous, 2 Idleness,
3 Nauseous, 4 Cerberus,
5 Hercules, 6 Reptiles, 7 Ellipsis,
8 Damascus, 9 Warriors,
10 Illinois, 11 Nowadays,
12 Goslings.
Answer: FINCH and REDWING

96

B	A	C	H	E	L	O	R
S	A	Y	O	N	A	R	A
V	I	C	T	O	R	I	A
O	N	L	O	O	K	E	R
T	R	A	V	E	S	T	Y
H	O	M	E	S	P	U	N
O	V	E	R	T	U	R	N
S	A	N	S	K	R	I	T

97

98

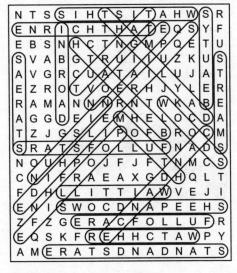

99

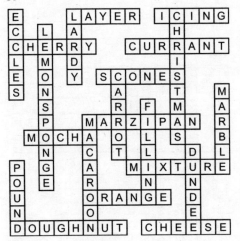

100

4	3	2	8	9	6	1	5	7
1	8	6	5	4	7	3	2	9
5	7	9	1	3	2	4	8	6
3	5	8	6	2	4	7	9	1
6	9	4	7	1	5	8	3	2
2	1	7	3	8	9	6	4	5
8	6	3	9	5	1	2	7	4
9	4	1	2	7	3	5	6	8
7	2	5	4	6	8	9	1	3

SOLUTIONS

101

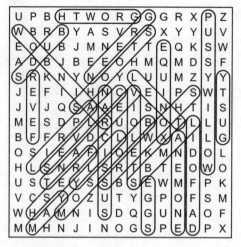

102

103

104

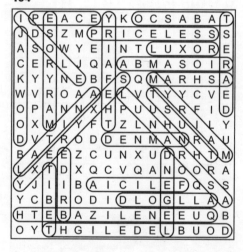

105

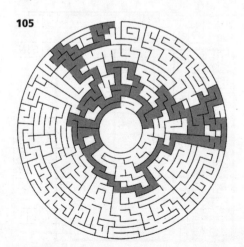

106

F: One of the apples is missing.

SOLUTIONS

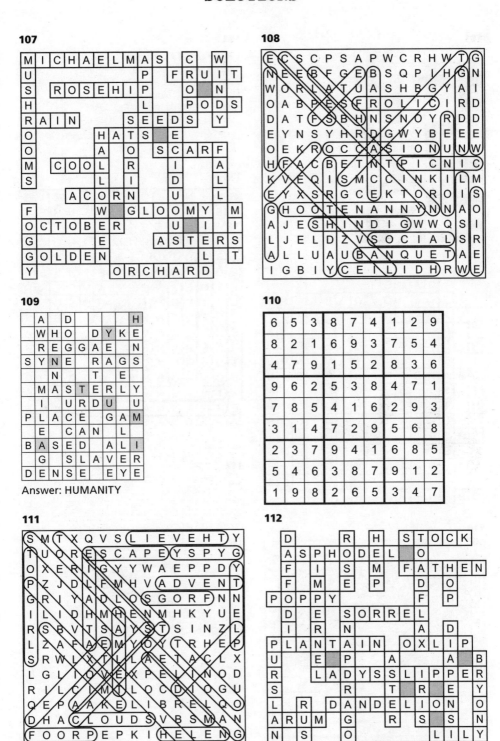

107

108

109

Answer: HUMANITY

110

111

112

SOLUTIONS

113

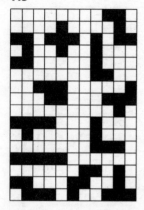

114

1 Raincoat, 2 Obedient, 3 Bankrupt,
4 Ignorant, 5 Nutrient, 6 Jubilant,
7 Argument, 8 Catapult, 9 Kilowatt,
10 Derelict, 11 Aircraft, 12 Wormcast.
Answer: ROBIN and JACKDAW

115

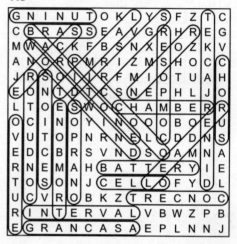

116

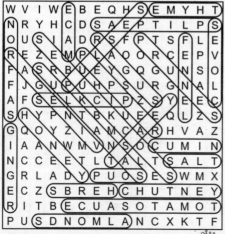

117

B and I

118

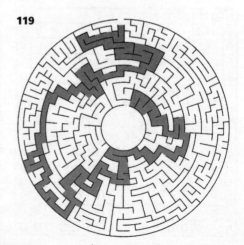

119

SOLUTIONS

120

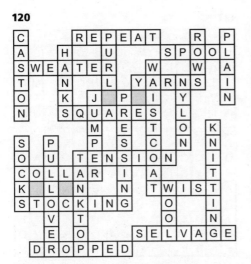

121

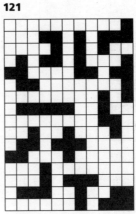

122

7	1	8	3	4	2	5	9	6
9	6	2	5	8	7	3	1	4
5	4	3	1	9	6	8	7	2
1	3	6	8	5	9	4	2	7
8	2	9	4	7	3	1	6	5
4	5	7	2	6	1	9	8	3
6	8	5	7	1	4	2	3	9
3	9	4	6	2	8	7	5	1
2	7	1	9	3	5	6	4	8

123

124

125

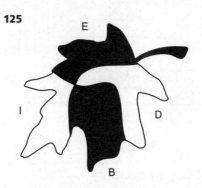

SOLUTIONS

126

S	O	U	R	S	O	P
S	P	U	R	R	E	Y
P	R	I	M	U	L	A
B	R	I	N	J	A	L
H	E	N	B	A	N	E
L	A	C	T	U	C	A
T	U	R	P	E	T	H

127

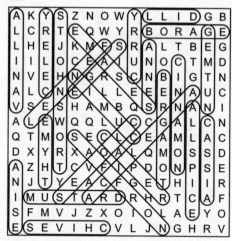

128

129

Answer: BRAMLEY

130

1 Language, 2 Immunise, 3 Nail file,
4 Necklace, 5 Everyone, 6 Tenerife,
7 Mandible, 8 Adequate, 9 Graduate,
10 Paradise, 11 Insulate, 12 Embezzle.
Answer: LINNET and MAGPIE

131

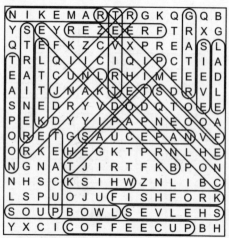

132

133

Nine-letters: ENJOYMENT

134

	A		I			A	B
	P	A	N	C	E	T	T	A
	I	T	S			L	L
N	A	M	E	P	L	A	T	E
	R		C	R	I	S	I	S
S	Y	S	T	E	M		C
	T		S	A	C	K	S
A	G	R	E	E		A	T
	L	I	S	T	E	N	E	R
C	A	P	S		K	I	W	I
	N	E	A	T	E	N	E	D
E	D	D	Y		S	E	R	E

Answer: DANCING

135

9	3	6	7	1	8	5	2	4
1	8	2	3	5	4	7	6	9
4	7	5	6	2	9	1	8	3
2	9	3	4	6	5	8	1	7
6	5	4	8	7	1	3	9	2
7	1	8	2	9	3	4	5	6
3	4	9	1	8	2	6	7	5
8	2	7	5	4	6	9	3	1
5	6	1	9	3	7	2	4	8

136

```
O N I K G N Y V G N B D A H M
W E H W P T O F O G N A M A Q
O D C M I B F M O N G B T Z F
X R R O X K E L M H O A F E B
N Z A B C L D E R I U Q I L E
A G E N H O A Q J Q S Z L N N
C S P O G T N Y M Y M R B U I
E N I G R E B U A A Z W E T T
P O L I V E K Q T P F A R P N
I L G X D J W J U R A Y T Z E
E E Q V I C T O R I A P L U M
N M U G O U Q A N C N D A T E
U H I A U H U I Y O J C X D L
R F L L U S D I F T L S E P C
P L G R A P E F R U I T U Z T
```

137

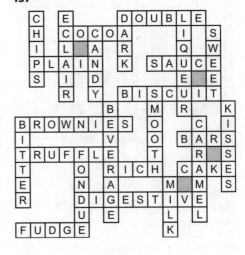

138

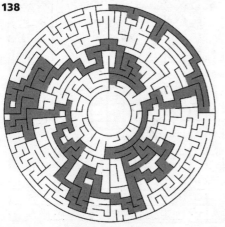

139

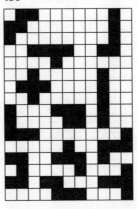

SOLUTIONS

140

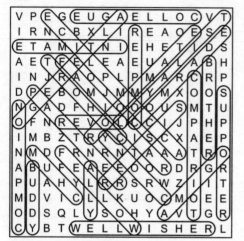

141

142

Answer: PEACOCK

143

H: One trail of melted wax is longer.

144

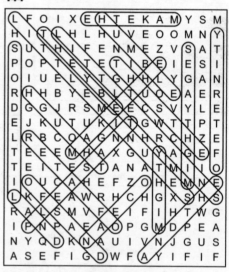

145

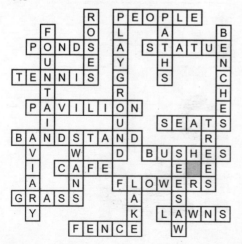

146

F	L	O	W	E	R	E	D
D	E	X	T	R	O	S	E
J	E	T	T	I	S	O	N
P	R	O	G	R	E	S	S
C	I	N	N	A	M	O	N
V	I	G	I	L	A	N	T
S	Q	U	I	R	R	E	L
A	M	E	T	H	Y	S	T